The Splendor of Easter

compiled and edited by

FLOYD W. THATCHER

WORD BOOKS, Publisher

Waco, Texas

Introduction

One day a man was walking along a dusty road in India pondering a deep personal problem. Suddenly, out of the corner of his eye he saw an ant hill, and stepping off the road, he watched the ants for quite some time. It seemed as if the entire hill was crawling as thousands of ants scurried about doing whatever ants do. He became fascinated with their busyness and stepped in closer so as to get a better look, but as he moved up, his shadow fell across the ant hill. Within moments every ant had disappeared into the hole. The hill was deserted. It was obvious that with their sun gone, danger lurked above, and in fright the ants had fled to the security of their hole.

Realizing what had happened the sensitive man was disturbed. He had meant no harm. It had not been his intention to step on the hill and crush thousands of ants. How could he reassure them? There was no way . . . unless he could become an ant—then he could communicate with them and they would understand.

Is this not a bit reminiscent of man's attitude toward God? For the most part God's encounter with man throughout the Old Testament produced fear responses. Even the Judean shepherds "were terrified" as "the glory of the Lord shone round them" and the angel choir announced the birth of the Savior who was Christ the Lord.

Floyd W. Thatcher, Vice President, Word, Incorporated; Executive Editor, Word Books, Publisher.

Again, on the first Easter morning the human response was one of fear. Mary of Magdala agonized in tears because they had stolen her Lord from the tomb, and the women were "terrified, frightened out of their wits" at the empty tomb. But the angel spoke, "There is no need for you to be afraid. I know you are looking for Jesus, who was crucified. He is not here for he is risen, as he said he would. Come and see the place where he lay, then go quickly and tell his disciples, he has risen from the dead. . . . Filled with awe and great joy the women came quickly away from the tomb. . ."

Fear transformed to great joy. God became man in the person of Jesus Christ—the communication process was complete, and we need no longer fear the shadow of God across the world. That is what Easter is all about.

And that is what this little book is all about. Here are fourteen short meditations or reflections, all focusing on history's most climactic event, the resurrection of Christ—the difference it made then and the difference it makes now in our struggle for meaning and acceptance in the somewhat sterile and impersonal environment of the 1970s. These may be read in a variety of ways, but possibly you will gain strength and purpose by reading one a day, beginning two weeks before Easter.

But however you read, the message remains the same. . .

There is no need for you to be afraid.
    He is not here, for he has risen from the dead. . . .
So let us thank God for giving us the victory
    through our Lord Jesus Christ.
Never give in then . . . never admit defeat;
    keep on working at the Lord's work always,
knowing that in the Lord,
    you cannot be laboring in vain.

Contents

EASTER

I shall tell you what Easter means;
To me, that is:
Not so many tulips and daffodils,
Bonnets and bunnies,
Baked hams and lambs.

It is the Creator suddenly bursting
The chrysalis in my heart,
With my consent,
Setting me free, uncongruously.
The words return: "If the
Son therefore shall set you free,
Ye shall be free indeed."

That's it! Freedom.
Freedom to live, to love,
And thus to give,
To take a glorious chance on life,
To be both liberated
And lost—in wonder.

I shall tell you what Easter means;
To me, that is:
The Eternal whispering, "Behold,
I am arisen in you,
Rising higher and higher,
Expanding enveloping.
Can you bear My being?
Courage, child."

Easter comes so many moons after
This or that,
But also, now and tomorrow.
I pray,
"In me arise, my Lord!
And keep on rising."

That is what Easter means;
To me, that is.

Sallie Chesham

1

Symbol of Living Hope

1 Peter 1:3–9

Easter took all of Christ's friends by surprise. Christ had warned them that he would rise from the dead, but they missed the meaning of his promise. And who wouldn't? We just don't expect the dead to rise. Nothing seems so permanent to us as death. It is inescapable.

I thought of this when I was in Winnipeg, Canada, speaking at the University of Manitoba and I heard a radio broadcast about Harry Houdini, the great escape artist. Maybe some of you who are older can remember seeing him or reading about his fantastic, incredible feats. Chained, handcuffed, he was locked in trunks and dumped into rivers, but he always managed to escape before drowning. But when appendicitis struck him in 1926, Harry Houdini, the great master of escape, could not struggle free from the chains of death.

David Allan Hubbard, President, Fuller Theological Seminary.

Death is inescapable. But Christ rose. That's why we have a New Testament; that's why we have a Christian Church. That first Easter, which took all of Jesus' disciples by storm, became the center of their thinking, their living, their preaching. Christ had escaped death and brought new hope to all men. That was their message.

To Peter, especially, the resurrection of Jesus was life-shaking. You can catch something of this excitement when you hear the opening words of his first letter: "Blessed be the God and Father of our Lord Jesus Christ. By his great mercy we have been born anew to a living hope through the resurrection of Jesus Christ from the dead."

Try to imagine the setting in which Peter was dictating those words. Silas, Paul's old traveling mate and Peter's comrade in ministry, was taking them down. The plain room with its rough furnishings must have vibrated with the exuberant words of the veteran apostles.

Let's suppose Peter and Silas had with them a younger companion, new to the faith, stretching his heart and mind to understand what the big fisherman was saying. Now we aren't sure that this was the case but let's imagine that it was.

We can picture him asking questions from time to time in his quest to wrap his mind around the wonders of the Christian way. He might be heard to say, "Peter, I've noticed how often you mention Jesus' resurrection. Just why is it so important to you?" "To understand why our Lord's resurrection is so important to me," Peter might respond, "you'd have to remember those dark hours before the first bright Easter morning. I was a kind of spokesman for the disciples. I had been with Jesus from the beginning of his ministry. When I met him, I left my boats and nets and everything and followed him.

12

"Then when he really needed me, I, Peter, who had made such bold confession of my faith and loyalty—I let him down. I actually denied that I was his follower—that I even knew him. I had been through storm and shipwreck—worked all night grappling with huge, teeming nets. My muscles were hardened through decades of labor. Look at my hands—you can still see the callouses from the oars and the burn marks from the ropes, yet I couldn't even look a wisp of a servant girl in the eye and confess my faith.

"Three times—I still feel sick when I think of it—three times I denied my Lord. And all the while he was getting ready to die for me. You can imagine how I felt about his execution."

Peter went on to say, "I had pinned all my hopes on him, and now he was dead. But worse still I had only bitter shame and dark futility to sustain me because of my total failure, my complete collapse under pressure.

"Then you can imagine how I felt when the women who had gone to the tomb with spices to help preserve his body brought the stunning news that his body was gone. But more than that, they said angels at the tomb had given them instructions to tell his disciples and Peter. Think what those words meant—and Peter. I was still part of the group. Jesus still wanted me to meet him with the others in Galilee.

"John and I ran as fast as we could to the tomb and went in. When our eyes got used to the dim light, we saw the grave clothes laid neatly aside and only the bare slab where his body had been placed. We saw with our own eyes that God had raised him from the dead. And everything was changed."

"What do you mean everything was changed, Peter?"

the young friend might ask. "I can see the joy Christ's resurrection brought you, but just how did it change you?" "By showing me that my destiny was certain," Peter could answer. "By demonstrating that my inheritance was assured."

"We have been born anew to an inheritance which is imperishable, undefiled, and unfading, kept in heaven" (1 Peter 1:4).

Peter might well point out the contrast which the resurrection brought about. "Think about my destiny and inheritance on that dark night when I refused to admit that I belonged to Jesus. I had left my home and business and had little to go back to, although I probably could have earned a living fishing." But who wants to go back to fishing when you have known the new life of love and power and service with Jesus? "For me, personally," Peter might say, "there was no sense of destiny, no assurance of an inheritance.

"All that I had I let slip through my fingers and I was left to feed on my failure. The one I believed in was dead and I had lost all faith in myself. Then the call to come and the empty tomb, and everything was changed. Jesus was alive, not dead. His call to me told me I was forgiven. The fractured pieces of my life began to come together. Man's great enemies—my great enemies—sin and death had more than met their match.

"Jesus had risen. Death was defeated. The dark wall which divides this life from the next was penetrated. Our destiny was assured, an inheritance with the Lord of glory—imperishable, undefiled, unfading—not dependent on someone's whim or fancy, not jeopardized by our weakness or failure. No force can put Jesus back in the tomb. No enemy can cheat us of our inheritance; it can't

14

be lost or stolen. It is kept for us and we for it by the fact that Christ rose from the dead."

"I see what you mean," Peter's young friend would say. "Christ's resurrection does make a difference—to you and to me. But if the future holds such glory and if Christ is victor over all his enemies why is there so much suffering now? And especially why are Christians being so severely persecuted for their faith? Why does the risen Christ allow it?"

"Let me put it this way," says Peter. "You are to keep rejoicing in the hope of your inheritance, though now for a little while you may have to suffer various trials, so that the genuineness of your faith, more precious than gold, which though perishable is tested by fire, may redound to praise and glory and honor at the revelation of Jesus Christ.

"Christ is interested in our growth, our character, our maturity. Like Job we may be asked to go through testings to prove that our love for God is not fleeting, that we are not fair-weather friends of Jesus Christ, that we serve him for what he is and not just what he gives.

"Yet at the same time, the resurrection tells us that suffering is temporary. We can take it and not let it destroy us or dash our hopes. Even when suffering drives us to the door of death we know that beyond that door stands the risen Christ, full of hope, waiting to receive us. We who trust him may lose a skirmish sometimes but he has already won the war. Suffering and hardship may take us to the mat, but they cannot pin us. Christ's cross tells us that God loves us enough to suffer for us. And his resurrection tells us that suffering can never have the last word for those who belong to him."

At this point Peter pauses and notes that his young

friend seems wistful and almost sad. "How can you wear such a puzzled, pensive face when we've been talking about the resurrection and the risen Christ?"

The friend says, "Now that I see how your life was changed by your contacts with Christ and especially with the risen Christ, I wish that I could have known him and loved him."

"What do you mean *wish?*" Peter breaks in. "You can. That's the point of the resurrection. He lives now as certainly, as vitally, as personally as he did then. Without having seen him you love him. Though you do not now see him you believe in him and rejoice with joy unspeakable and full of glory. As the outcome of your faith, you obtain the salvation of your soul."

We can see now why praise and adoration poured forth from Peter's heart as he dictated these first verses of his letter. No wonder he said, "Blessed be the God and Father of our Lord Jesus Christ." The resurrection meant to him a sure inheritance, encouragement in suffering, and the joy of constant friendship with his Savior. For Peter the resurrection was an historical fact. He was there when it happened. For Peter the resurrection was history-making. It changed his history, his destiny, his ministry.

Christ is risen. That's history. Christ is risen for you. That's history-making.

2

To See Each Other "Real" Is Resurrection

Luke 24:13–35

Recently I was sitting on the patio in front of our home with some friends when a neighbor appeared and spoke a word of greeting very solemnly.

Something was wrong; I knew. I got up, followed him a few steps away, and he said, "Have you heard what's happened to our family?" I replied, "No." He seemed unable to continue, so I asked, "Is it Ann?" "No." "One of the children?" "No." Then he said, "It's our two-year-old grandson, Chappie. He was drowned in the swimming pool yesterday afternoon."

I walked with him as he told me what had happened, and we went into his house. His wife was there, cooking, furiously cooking. We talked, as people talk. And I said, "I believe in the resurrection." And his wife said, "I believe in the resurrection, too, but I don't understand it."

Robert A. Raines, Senior Minister, First Community Church, Columbus, Ohio.

How should we who believe in the resurrection understand it? How can we understand it? Well, we can begin
by going with those two men up the road to Emmaus that
Easter afternoon. Their world was smashed like the world
of my neighbors. The little band of disciples were scattering to their homes. There just wasn't anywhere else
to go.

While walking along, the two on the road to Emmaus
were joined by a stranger who asked what they were dis-
cussing so intently. In amazement Cleopas responded,
"Are you the only visitor to Jerusalem who doesn't know
the things that happened there?" The visitor said, "What
things?" In response, they told the stranger the story of
Jesus, and concluded with, "We had hoped that he was
the one to redeem Israel." We had hoped—oh, we hoped
so much—we dreamed about a new kind of world with
him. We had great hopes—but no more, for he's gone and
our hopes have gone with him.

Upon arriving in Emmaus, they persuaded the stranger
to stay with them for dinner. As they sat at table they
watched him bless and break the bread. Those familiar
hands—his hands! It was Jesus—and even as they saw him
and knew him, he was gone—vanished out of their sight,
leaving them in guilty surprise with blank misgivings of
a creature moving about in worlds not realized. Return-
ing immediately to Jerusalem they found the other disciples gathered together there, aflame with the incredible
news that Christ had appeared to Peter. They told what
had happened to them on the road and how they had
recognized him in the breaking of the bread.

Now, something happened to those disciples—something whose consequences have affected and changed the
history of the world more than any other single chain of

events. What did happen? How can we understand it? The one overriding historical fact we can get our hands on is this—the fact of the Easter faith of the disciples. They believed, whether hallucinated, deluded, or in truth. They believed that their friend and teacher, Jesus, had appeared to them alive after his death, that he had risen from the dead. And the change in those men was radical— hot witness of a group of men who now were ready to die for him who had died for them. Their message was clear and unmistakable. This Jesus whom men had crucified, God has raised from the dead. God has vindicated his life and his work. Sin and death are beaten, are destroyed. Believe in him, he forgives you, he gives you new life. Come with us, and live with him.

It was Paul who defined the crucial significance of this resurrection event, when he said in a letter to the Corinthians, "If Christ has not been raised, your faith is futile." Paul was right historically. If the resurrection event had not occurred, there would have been no church of Jesus Christ and no Scriptures.

Paul was right theologically. If Christ, in fact, has not been raised from the dead, sin and death remain victorious over us and we are eternally bound by them, and the church is not built on a rock of reality but on sands of superstition. It is one or the other—superstition or reality. It is of such importance that we are not allowed neutrality or indifference, but only faith or unbelief. But, in fact, says Paul, Christ has been raised from the dead, the first fruits of those who have fallen asleep. Something utterly new in time, space, and history has occurred; the hour-glass of history has turned. This resurrection is not just a curtain call after the drama of redemption has been played out. It sounds the trumpet of a new drama, a new creation as provocative as the first, and explosion of new life here and hereafter for us and all the world.

Once again, it is Paul who gives us both the earliest and the most significant documentary testimony to the resurrection of Christ. Writing in the 50s (and you recall, the Gospels came many years later), Paul says to the Corinthians, "I deliver to you as of first importance what I also received, that Christ died for our sins . . ., that he was buried, and that he was raised on the third day . . . that he appeared to Peter, then he appeared to the twelve. Then he appeared to more than five hundred brethren. . . . Then he appeared to James, then he appeared to all the apostles. Last of all, ... he appeared also to me." Note closely, Paul uses one word, the word "appeared," the same word to describe all these encounters of men with the risen Christ, including his on the Damascus Road—implying surely that his own encounter was as valid and authentic as theirs, and further, that it was of the same order and character and manner as theirs.

Clearly, the risen Christ who met Paul on the Damascus Road did not come in physical form but in spiritual form, a tangible spiritual presence, able to communicate, but not bound by conditions of time, space, history. Indeed, in this same chapter Paul insists flesh and blood cannot inherit the kingdom of God, and he uses the phrases "spiritual body," "glorified body" to speak of the body of the resurrection. The appearance of the risen Christ to the two men in the restaurant was of this same order, a tangible spiritual presence.

Jesus came, as he always comes, as a stranger to Mary in the garden, who thought he was the gardener; to Peter on the beach, who thought he was another fisherman; to the two men on the road, who thought he was a visitor to Jerusalem. Clearly, if he had come in resuscitated flesh, he would have been immediately recognizable and recognized. That he wasn't is not due to the dimness of the light or the preoccupation of the disciples, but to the nature of the resurrection body itself, for the risen Christ was not like us. He came incognito, appeared and vanished. He was in, but no longer of this world. As Eliot anguishes to express this inexpressible reality, ". . . neither flesh nor fleshless, both a new world and the old made explicit, understood in the completion of its partial ecstasy, resolution of its partial horror, past and future woven together in the weakness of the changing body." He came as a stranger, and they recognized him because they loved him. He reveals himself now and then only to those who love him—to Mary, who recognized his voice; to Peter, who recognized his unique authority in the catch of fish; to those two men, who recognized his familiar hands. When they saw him in the restaurant, they wanted to hold on to him, to grasp him, but he vanished from their sight.

We can never grasp God. Whenever we glimpse eternity, see through the mortal curtain, we are already beyond science into being, beyond knowledge into faith, and we know the holy vision but we cannot see it any more. We cannot storm the citadel of God with all our powers of reason, and find him out, for he reveals himself to us in a total confrontation of the whole man in an encounter with the living Christ. And then it is less true that we comprehend him, and more true that he apprehends us in a moment of guilty surprise, with blank misgivings—creatures moving about in worlds not realized.

We are like the artist, William Morris, who was commissioned to paint Jane Burdan. He spent several hours before the canvas and finally showed it to her—and it was blank except for the words, "I cannot paint you, but I love you." When we love Jesus, the risen Christ, we may not be able to paint him or to write poetry about him, but we are able to see him alive in the world. We are able to recognize him. It's his Easter gift. We can recognize him now in a stranger on the road, in a restaurant, in the sick, the hungry, the thirsty ("I thirst"). His Easter gift to us is the capacity to see him in other persons.

One who had the rare privilege of being the friend of Forbes Robertson said of him, "He saw in each of us, however unlovely our lives, something, somewhere, of Jesus Christ." To be an Easter Christian is to see something, somewhere, of Jesus Christ in every person you meet and come to love, for love has its own peculiar vision. When you do love another person, you see something of Christ in him—you see a beauty that nobody else can see, that is opened, unfolded, given only to love. You see a marvel, a greatness, a treasure, a grandeur, a unique possibility hidden to the ordinary view. And, you know, we need now and then when we see a beauty and a marvel in each other, to tell each other about it, because sometimes the last person to know that Christ is alive in a man is the man himself. And to know it is a resurrection. To be an Easter Christian is to be a catcher of souls—a "Catcher in the Rye," on the road, in the restaurant. It is to be a looker for the lost, a finder of the lonely, a liberator of the captive. It is to see the whole human family with new eyes, to love each person you see.

Recently a telegram was delivered to me, and as I opened it, I thought possibly it was from my father and mother, but it was datelined Omsk, in Russia. It was in Russian and I couldn't read it. It was sent by Bishop

Nicholai, one of the delegation of Russian churchmen who visited this country several years ago. He and two others stayed overnight in our home, and every Christmas and Easter since he has sent some kind of greeting, but this was the first time a telegram had arrived on Easter Sunday. Here is a man who is an Easter Christian, a Russian. Jesus Christ lives in him and in millions of other Russians, and Chinese, and Vietnamese, and people all over the world.

George Bernanos, a parish priest, writes words which open up the world for us, and as you read them, think about yourself, your family, your friends, the people you have come to know and see this past year. He says, "This morning I prayed hard for my parish, my poor parish. The words cannot even be spoken without a kind of soaring love. I know that my parish is a reality, that we belong to each other for eternity, but if only the good God would open my eyes that I might behold the face of my parish. The face of my parish, the look in the eyes—they must be gentle and suffering, patient eyes like mine when I cease struggling and let myself be borne along the great invisible flux that sweeps us all helter-skelter, the living and the dead, into the deep waters of eternity. They would be the eyes of all parishes, perhaps of the poor human race itself. Our Lord saw them from the cross—'Father, forgive them; for they know not what they do.'"

God is taking the bare threads of our little lives and weaving a tapestry of such beauty and glory as we cannot possibly imagine. When for a moment he enables us to see through the mortal curtain, face to face, Christ in each other, such love is raised up within us as makes us choke with Easter joy.

In the play, "The Rain Maker," Lizzie, the daughter,

speaks to a friend about her father, and says, "Some nights I am in the kitchen washing the dishes, and Pop is playing poker with the boys. Well, I'll watch him real close, and at first I'll just see an ordinary, middle-aged man, not very interesting to look at. And then, minute by minute, I'll see little things I never saw before—good things and bad things, queer little habits I never noticed he had, ways of talking I'd never paid any mind to. Suddenly I know who he is, and I love him so much I could cry, and I thank God I took the time to see him real."

To see each other *real,* now and then, is resurrection!

3

The Easter Faith:
Fact or Fable

Today we stand at that holy season of the year when throughout the world Christians are rejoicing in the central fact of our faith that Jesus Christ is risen.

The French thinker, Auguste Comte, once told Thomas Carlyle that he was going to start a new religion that would replace Christianity. "Very good," replied Carlyle. "All you will have to do is to be crucified, rise again the third day, and get the world to believe you are still alive. Then your new religion will have a chance."

From the very first Easter until now the Christian faith has moved forward based on the fact that Jesus Christ did rise from the dead and the fact that he is alive and changing lives. Whenever people met the historic Jesus, they were changed. And this transforming influence of Jesus Christ did not fade out in the first century. Ever since it has left a trail of changed lives.

Leighton Ford, Evangelist, Billy Graham Evangelistic Association.

I know a vicious gang leader in Harlem who has now become a preacher of the Good News that God is love. I have heard a savage Indian chief in South America who butchered the missionaries who came to tell him about God, but who now is the leader of the church in his tribe. I once met a prize-winning biochemist at the University of Minnesota who had a profound Christian experience when he was fifty years old and deeply influenced his colleagues by the way that he calmly faced death by cancer. And I can think of thousands of others. To the Christian these changed lives are evidence that Jesus Christ is indeed alive.

However, the skeptic believes that this resurrection faith is not fact. He says it's fable. He is convinced that these changed lives can be explained psychologically and that we are just deluding ourselves as Christians into believing in God.

Several years ago during a meeting at the University of Georgia a young male student challenged me, "You say your God is real. But isn't this just your idea? What if I said that lamp over in the corner was God?"

I told him that the lamp had never communicated with me but that God had. But he persisted, "If you really believed that lamp was God, maybe you'd get the same results!"

A new religion has emerged among skeptics in our day that could be called "nothing but." It says that our Christian faith is "nothing but" wishful thinking. If a teenager is converted, it is "nothing but" a phase of adolescence. If an older person is converted, it is "nothing but" senility and aging. Martin Luther's faith, to this new religion of skepticism, was "nothing but" the result of a neurotic personality. St. Augustine's conversion to Christianity was "nothing but" his attempt to regain the love of his mother which he had lost during his wild youth. Sin is "nothing but" a psychological hang-up. Conversion is "nothing but" a quirk of the maladjusted. In short, our whole faith can be explained away psychologically, so they say.

Way back in the first century that same accusation was leveled at Paul the Apostle. A critic said that his religion had driven him crazy and was "nothing but" a delusion. Paul had been arrested in Jerusalem on a trumped-up charge of disturbing the peace. He was given a hearing before Festus, who was a Roman official, and Agrippa, who was a Jewish king.

As recorded in Acts 26 Paul made his defense with simple and burning eloquence. He told how he had been raised as a devout Jew, how he had become a Pharisee, how he had opposed the teachings of Jesus, but how one day as he was on the way to hunt out and arrest the Christians in the city of Damascus Jesus actually appeared to him and from that point Paul became his messenger to the world to tell all men that Jesus had died but he was alive again.

At this point the Roman governor, Festus, burst out, "You're mad, Paul, you are mad! All this study is driving you crazy!" (Cf. verse 24, Williams).

But Paul replied, "I am not mad, Your Excellency. What I am saying is sober truth" (verse 25, NEB).

That same accusation that was leveled at Paul is made today against the Christian. Our testimony to the reality of our Christian experience is explained away. Some say it is merely the result of conditioning; we have been taught since childhood to think and act like Christians, so we do. Others say that Christian experience is just an illusion that fulfills a psychological need in our lives.

Now of course there are answers to these charges. If it takes conditioning to make a Christian, then how do you explain the tens of thousands who became Christians who had no Christian upbringing? When the skeptic says that we need a father image and that we just make up a God to replace the father image of our childhood and give us a feeling of security, we can answer that maybe he is an atheist just because he is rejecting the daddy that he hated when he was a boy!

Still, these questions make people wonder. Am I dreaming the whole thing? Is my faith just a wish fulfillment? Is Christian experience for real? Or is it all in my mind?

Now here is where the fact of the historical resurrection of Jesus Christ that we remember at Easter is so important. Sometimes we sing:

> He lives, He lives,
> Christ Jesus lives today. . . .
> You ask me how I know He lives?
> He lives within my heart.

That is wonderful, but it is only half the story. I know today that Jesus lives not just because I have experienced him in my heart but I know because of what happened in history.

Read the twenty-sixth chapter of Acts and you will find that is exactly the point that Paul made when Festus accused him of being crazy and deluded. He answered by tying his faith and his experience in to the fact of the resurrection.

First, Paul raised a *philosophical question*. He asked King Agrippa, "Why is it thought incredible by any of you that God raises the dead?" (verse 8, RSV). Now if there is no God, obviously he could raise nobody. But if

28

God is and if God is the free, sovereign, and all-powerful God revealed in the Bible, then certainly he can intervene in the world he has made. So why is it incredible that God should raise the dead?

"Well," you may object, "in the age of science surely we can't believe that a dead man can rise again."

Why not? Science can't rule out the possibility of the resurrection, simply because the resurrection is a unique event and science does not deal with unique events. The only things that science measures are the things that can be repeated over and over and over again.

"Well," you may protest, "I just can't help it. No matter what the evidence is, I just couldn't believe, for example, that my neighbor down the street, Tom Smith, could be dead for many hours and then come alive."

But we are not talking about your neighbor, Tom Smith, are we? We are talking about One who was unique, a Christ who was unique in his life and unique in his teaching and unique in his personality and unique in his sinlessness and unique as the very Son of God. Is it really unbelievable that he should also be unique in his resurrection?

If you find that you can't believe that Jesus Christ really came back from the dead, you should in all honesty ask, "Is my problem merely intellectual? Or is it possible that I don't want it to be true?"

Then Paul raised a *biblical question.* He made it clear to King Agrippa that he had not cooked up some novel theory, that the only thing he was declaring was what was promised in the Old Testament—that the Messiah would come, that he would die, that he would rise again and be a light to all men everywhere, and that these predictions were fulfilled in Jesus Christ (verses 22, 23).

29

"King Agrippa," asked Paul, "do you believe the prophets? I know that you believe (them)" (verse 27, RSV). Paul was saying, "If you believe the prophets and if you compare their predictions with the historical facts about Jesus Christ, then you have to acknowledge that Christianity is true."

In the Old Testament there were some three hundred distinct prophecies of Jesus Christ that lay like the pieces of a jigsaw puzzle. They didn't quite fit until Jesus came and put them together.

Dr. Peter Stoner, who was chairman of the departments of astronomy and mathematics and engineering at Pasadena City College, worked with over six hundred students for several years applying the "principle of probability" to Bible prophecy. As an example, they took eight prophecies of the Old Testament concerning Jesus and estimated that the chances of all these being fulfilled in one man in one lifetime simply by chance were one in ten followed by thirty-two zeros! That is why when we see Christ by his resurrection fulfilling the Old Testament, it's a further confirmation that the Bible is true.

Then Paul also defended his experience with *historical evidence.* He insisted to King Agrippa, "What I am saying is sober truth. The king is well versed in these matters, and I can speak freely to him. I do not believe he can be unaware of any of these facts" (cf. verses 25, 26, NEB), "for," he said, "this was not done in a corner" (verse 26, RSV). In other words, Paul was pointing out that the facts about Jesus were a matter of public record. They were a matter of common knowledge. All over Jerusalem the Christians had proclaimed his life and his death and his resurrection, and thousands had believed these facts and no one tried to refute them.

You see, if somebody came to me today and said, "Mr. Ford, you've just fooled yourself into believing that Jesus Christ has changed your life. That is just a feeling that you have," I'd answer like this, "Yes, I know that Jesus Christ is living because of what he has done in my life, but that's only part of the story. The other vital part is that I know that Jesus Christ is living because he rose in history."

Several months ago a very unusual meeting took place at Harvard University. Hundreds of students gathered to hear an address by Professor J. N. D. Anderson, who is dean of the faculty of law at the University of London. His brilliant address surveyed the evidence for the resurrection of Jesus from the eyes of a lawyer. He smashed many of the theories which have tried to explain away the resurrection of Jesus Christ. And then he closed his address by listing a series of historic facts that must be explained in some other way if the resurrection didn't happen.

If there were no resurrection, he asked, how do you explain the Christian Church that can be traced back to the first century? The New Testament says it began because its Founder was raised from the dead. Is there any other theory that fits the facts?

How do you explain the success of the early Church? he asked. How did the apostles make thousands of converts in Jerusalem by preaching the resurrection when anyone who wanted to check out the tomb to see if Jesus were still dead and buried could have done so simply by taking a short walk?

What changed the apostles? he asked. What changed Peter from a man who denied Jesus three times before the Cross to someone who defied the chief priests after the resurrection? What happened to James, the brother of Jesus? During Jesus' lifetime he didn't believe in him, but he became a leader of the church in Jerusalem after the resurrection. What changed Paul from persecutor to apostle of Christ?

You see, as Paul said, "this thing was not done in a corner" (verse 26). The documents are there to examine. The evidence is there to consider. And I challenge you today, if you will not and cannot accept the resurrection, what explanation can you give?

The final thrust of Paul's appeal to King Agrippa was his *personal evidence.* Agrippa was embarrassed when Paul asked if he believed the prophets, and he scoffed, "Paul, you think it will not take much to win me over and make a Christian of me." But Paul answered, "I wish to God that not only you, but all those also who are listening to me today, might become what I am, apart from these chains" (verses 28, 29, NEB).

Here is our final appeal to you as Christians, "Taste and see that the Lord is good" (Ps. 34:8). Try him, and you will find that he can do for you what he has done for us. Jesus Christ has given us purpose and meaning in a world that is empty and without direction. He has given us power to do right in a society that is going through a profound moral power failure. He has given us the solution to the guilt problem with his forgiveness purchased at his Cross. He has given us a family with God as our Father and other Christians as our brothers and sisters in a world that is increasingly lonely.

It was the living Christ who transformed the life of evangelist Lane Adams. He was a nightclub entertainer whose life was slowly caving in. Then he began reading a Bible in a Louisville motel room. And suddenly one day

32

as he was reading the story of the risen Christ showing himself to doubting Thomas, Lane turned to his wife and said, "This Jesus Christ is alive someplace. I'm going to find him!" He did—and today he is a living witness to the reality of the living Christ.

This same Christ, the One who intercepted Paul two thousand years ago, is reaching into your life today. Do you sense that he is speaking to you, offering to bring sense and fulfillment to the loneliness and lostness of your life? Then why don't you make the great experiment of faith? Let the resurrection happen in you. Open your life to this living Christ and discover for yourself that Jesus Christ is for real and that he is the answer to the questions of your life.

4

Amazing Grace

John 1:17

Some years ago Dr. Fritz Kunkel was giving a series of lectures at my seminary, the Pacific School of Religion in Berkeley, California. One night my sister-in-law went with me to hear him, and after that very wise psychologist had finished his lecture and we were on our way home, she said with a kind of wonderment, "Why, that man knew exactly how I feel and what my problems are. It is a miracle."

Something of that same feeling was mine upon reading the words of John Newton's "Amazing Grace." Here is my spiritual biography—in that old hymn, beloved of the church, there is written the story of my spiritual life and experience. It is the greatest hymn in the church and nobody can make me believe that a generation is bad that places it at the top of the list of its favorite songs. I am

Gerald Kennedy, Bishop, The United Methodist Church.

using John Newton's verses as the outline of our Easter thought.

First there is a sense of divine wonder and awe at what God has done for us through Christ. Did I deserve this experience? Was there anything I could have done to earn it? Of course not! Here is what Newton said,

> Amazing grace! How sweet the sound
> That saved a wretch like me!
> I once was lost, but now am found,
> Was blind, but now I see.

At the root of the Christian experience there is this deep sense of amazement that my poor life has received this gift. The tragedy of our time is that men have lost the sense of wonder. The scientifically minded generation begins to consider all of living as a logical thing to be analyzed and given naturalistic explanation and definition. It is a sad thing that the wonder of it all so often passes us by. The artist and the poet live under the influence of a constant surprise. The Christian always stands in awe before the God of Wonder and Miracle from whom Jesus is the supreme revelation. The boredom of modern living is the inevitable result for men who have lost their sense of his presence.

All too often the church has become for us a mere organization and our part in it is a tiresome round of meetings which we participate in because of a sense of duty. However, in reality the church is that fellowship of men who remember Jesus and are overwhelmed with a sense of the wonder of it all. And the evangelism of the church is finding the method to share this wonder with men who have not experienced it. The enemy of the church is simply dullness and boredom, and when in our heart there is rekindled this sense of "the amazing grace" that has come to us through him, we are made alive.

Sometime ago in the church where I preach a couple of times a month, my young associate spoke to me about having a "contemporary service." The young people had commissioned him to approach me about it. I thought it was a great idea. But the director of the choir would have no part of it. He could not see that guitars were better than the pipe organ. I saw his point and suggested that on that morning he could visit another church.

So, we had a group of young people singing a modern folk song or two for the anthem, and they were accompanied by several guitars. My associate prayed in the language of youth. I preached that morning, and that was the only "square" thing in the service. We even had some very talented young people do an interpretive dance before the altar.

At the close of the service I went down to greet the people as is my custom. I saw coming toward me an elderly lady who was very well-to-do and very generous to the church. I thought I saw fire in her eye and looked around desperately for a means of escape. But there was no place and I waited to meet her attack with what grace I could muster. To my surprise she said to me, "Bishop, I have not felt such joy and excitement in a service since the old days of revival meetings which I attended fifty years ago as a young girl. Let's do it again." And it came to me that what people want when they are asking for contemporary services, is simply that it should be alive and full of the wonder of amazing grace. Whether the service is traditional or contemporary is not the point. What is important is that the service should be filled with a sense that worship is not a routine matter but is a celebration of the wonderful thing God has done for us.

What a word this is for the preacher! If preaching is a synonym for dullness and has become merely explanation or commentary, it has forgotten that the gospel means "good news." It does not need to be optimistic news or a lullaby from the pulpit. But it must be filled with the good news that our salvation is a gift of the amazing grace of Christ. Everybody I meet is having a hard time and life is not easy for any human being. But through it all there is the divine sense of a miracle and a gift unspeakable and full of glory. The Bible is full of this story and the climax of it all is in the amazing grace that Jesus Christ brings to us.

When I look back over my own life, I can never doubt but that I, too, have been given the gift of the amazing grace. To become a preacher in the church and commissioned to tell people the good news is more than any man can ever deserve.

St. Francis and Roger Bacon, the great scientist, were different in some ways, but both men were Christians in an age that had forgotten the nature of true Christianity. Roger Bacon said, "I will conduct my experiments on the magnetic forces of the lodestone at the self-same shrine where my fellow scientist, St. Francis, performed his experiments on the magnetic forces of love." Both of those men had the same spirit. If we become wise enough, we, too, shall discover that science and religion are united in their spirit of wonder as they stand in the presence of God whose gift of grace overwhelms us with awe. But it is the Christian faith that keeps that spirit alive in the heart of Christians.

The second thing that comes to us out of this hymn is divine guidance for living. John Newton writes:

'Twas grace that taught my heart to fear,
And grace my fears relieved;
How precious did that grace appear
The hour I first believed!

Now there is much teaching about divine guidance that I have not experienced and I do not believe. When I was a young preacher, I was invited to the home of a very wealthy man one night to meet some leaders of the Oxford Group who were to testify. My friend was much impressed that they had something that might revive the church. I sat and listened to men describe things I had never experienced. One of the men was a salesman, and he said that he always knew when and where to call on a prospect. His time was saved by not going to places where nobody was home or where no one was interested in what he sold. I listened much troubled and decided I was not a very good Christian for I had missed this experience those people said should come to every Christian.

A good many years have passed since that time and I must confess that I have never experienced guidance of that kind. There are so many times when I do not know the way. There are so many times when the road takes an unexpected turn and I am not sure what the outcome will be. And there have been so many times when I have talked to a person about Christ and did not get through to him.

An old friend of mine said to me one time, "All my prayers have been answered. I never prayed a prayer that was not answered, but usually the Lord said no." And I must confess that oftentimes he has answered my prayers that same way.

Yet, I cannot help but feel divine guidance in my living. So many horrible things could have happened but I have been spared. There is so much tragedy of life that has come to people because of wrong choices. I am not so good that I always make the right choices, but God has guided my steps past the moral debacles. I wake every morning with a sense that the day will be full of great experiences and dangers but that in him I have a sure guide.

He guides me through a sense of duty. How many times I have been faced with the feeling, "You ought to do this." It is usually an uncomfortable feeling, but always when I bring myself around to doing what I do not want to do, I have been led on the right way at the right time. The more I think of this pressure that comes from obligation, the more I come to the conclusion that it is God's guidance.

He guides through discipline. There was a time when I thought that heaven was a place where you could sleep as late as you wanted to in the morning. After I had been in the pastorate for a time, it came to me that I had to have some time either after everyone had gone to bed or before they got up in the morning. If a preacher takes his job seriously, he knows that somewhere along his schedule he has to plan for a period when he can be by himself. For all these years, I have gotten up early though I never liked it. It begins to dawn upon me after more than thirty years that he has guided my life through that discipline. A generation that wants always to "do its own thing" usually means to do as it pleases. It will learn that without discipline life becomes sloppy and unbuttoned.

Ultimately the sense of direction comes from God. John Newton never doubted that God's hand guided him "to fear," and it was the same hand which guided him to confidence after he had "first believed." Nor do I doubt that the grace of the Lord Jesus Christ has been as an all-pervading influence pointing in the right direction.

Edward Barrett, dean of the Pulitzer School of Journalism, defined the newspaper writer's task: "The key journalist of the future must be able to relate today's event to yesterday's fact in the way that helps indicate tomorrow's meaning." So, the Christian finds that each day's event is interpreted and given meaning when it is related and interpreted by the experience of God's grace.

The third thing the hymn says is that experience comes to us through Christ and that experience has great authority.

> Through many dangers, toils, and snares,
> I have already come;
> 'Tis grace has brought me safe thus far,
> And grace will lead me home.

Life is a very dangerous experience. When I was a college student, I had a summer job supervising a playground. It scared me to death because I realized for the first time that if children do not have someone looking after them, they will never make it. I kept saying to myself, "How in the world can these youngsters be brought to adulthood? Look at all the chances they take and how unaware they seem to be of the dangerous things they do. How can I be sure of getting them through this day safely?" But they were unaware of my fears and somehow, they made it.

The father of four children came home after a hard

40

day in his office. He said to his wife, "Don't give me any bad news. If you haven't some good news, please don't say anything. I am worn out." His wife said sweetly, "Well, I do have good news for you. Three of your four children didn't break their arms today." That is why parents, and mothers in particular, worry, and why shouldn't they? So John Newton, looking at the many narrow escapes he has had, simply concludes that it was grace that has brought him safe thus far and it is grace that will lead him home.

This is the great emphasis of our faith. John Wesley could write of his Aldersgate experience, "I felt my heart strangely warmed." After that great moment he said that he felt even his own sins were forgiven. He became a man of spiritual power. Others could talk about religion and describe it as it ought to be or as it was in some places, but he had this note of authority. John Newton was saying in effect that he, too, knew the experience of being brought through the "dangers, toils and snares." It is the word of the New Testament and the witness of our Lord that God makes himself known and a man may have that experience.

What can I say about our own experience? Let me say, for one thing, that the passing years have brought me the assurance that the Christian faith is the only way a man can live. When I hear about a new morality, I smile and think to myself that there is no more a new morality than there is a new law of gravitation. Morality is written deep into the nature of things, and I have a choice of adjusting my life to the moral precepts and living or defying them and dying. All about me are examples of men who have taken another way, of nations that have broken the moral law, and of societies that have tried to substitute something new by law. I stand today utterly convinced that Christianity is the way of life and its denial leads only to death.

I have become convinced that Jesus was right. That simple affirmation is the heart of my theology. There are some hard sayings in the Bible, but experience tells me that I had better come to terms with them or reap sorrow. Jesus is not just a poetic, dreaming man who said some very nice things about human relationships. He is the world's supreme realist who reveals reality. In the life of Jesus Christ and in his teachings, we have the great revelation of the way things are. I stand on that as if it were a rock, and I find that my experience tells me that it is truth.

When John Newton was an old man, he was still preaching this faith that sprang out of his own experience. He was not what we would call a great preacher. But the simplicity of his life and affirmations found men and they came to hear him. They felt that there was a saintliness about him and an authority in his life which in this hymn of his he reveals sprang out of his experience. As they said of a far greater than Newton, "He speaks as one who has authority."

George Kauffman sat one evening talking with Edna Ferber and he announced suddenly that he was thinking of killing himself. Deeply shocked, Edna Ferber asked, "How, George?" Kauffman answered amiably, "With kindness." Oh, the kindness of that amazing grace that has found me through all of my past life and gives me trust for the future!

The last thing the hymn speaks about is faith.

The Lord has promised good to me,

42

His word my hope secures;
He will my shield and portion be
As long as life endures.

This seems to me to be the perfect statement of the meaning of faith. Did John Newton have some special knowledge about the future and what was in store for him? He had no more than any man has—for him as for everyone else, the future was an unknown experience. But he takes refuge in the promises of the Lord and the hope he has that springs from his previous experience. He has done all this thus far, John Newton could say, and the Lord has been faithful to the promises he has made. So he could bet his life that the future was safe on the basis of what had gone before. This is faith.

We live by faith—no man could exist five minutes on just what he can prove. Could Newton prove it? Of course not. But he was saved by faith and this all-pervading grace. So am I and so are you. That is why the longer a man follows him, the more certain he is about the future.

A popular idea of faith today is that it has something to do with believing things that are unbelievable for the tough-minded. The late Philip Wylie sometimes intimated that this was all right for soft-minded people, but for realists like himself, it was not enough. Nothing could show more clearly our misunderstanding of what Christians mean by faith.

Paul had the truth of it when he spoke of faith as the act of response. Faith is a man saying yes to God, and it is a man's response to something for which there can be no proof. It is Christian faith when we respond to the great mysteries of life.

God is man's great adventure. He calls us to risk something because of our faith in him. When we speak of being "saved by faith," we mean that we dare to risk for God. The things a man can prove are relatively insignificant, and life is built upon the great things which find us and which cannot be proved. John Newton's great hymn dares to say that the word of God secures his hope and that faith in him will be his shield and portion as long as his life endures.

One hundred and seventy-one years ago in Vermont a man named John Todd was born. In a little while his family moved to the small community of Killingsworth, Connecticut. Before he was six years old, he was made an orphan by the death of both his father and mother. He and his brothers and sisters were sent out among relatives to be brought up. John was assigned to a kind-hearted aunt who lived about ten miles away. She was both his father and his mother and saw him all the way through Yale College and into his chosen profession. Years later she was taken seriously ill and knew that she was close to death. She was afraid to die and uncertain about the experience she had to face. In her anxiety and distress she wrote to John who had been more like a son to her than a nephew. Since he couldn't go to her bedside, he wrote her this letter:

It is now nearly thirty-five years since I, a little boy of six, was left quite alone in the world . . . I have never forgotten the day when I made the long journey to your house in North Killingsworth. I still recall my disappointment when instead of coming for me yourself you sent your hired man Caesar to fetch me. And I can still remember my tears and anxiety, as perched on your horse and clinging tightly to Caesar, I started out for my new home. As we rode along, I became more and more afraid and finally said anxiously to Caesar, "Do you think she will go to bed before we get there?" "Oh, no," he answered reassuringly, "she'll sure stay up for you. When we get out of these here woods, you will see her candle shining in the window."

Presently we did ride out into a clearing, and there, sure enough, was your candle. I remember you were waiting at the door, that you put your arms around me, that you lifted me down from the horse. There was a fire on your hearth, a warm supper on your stove. After supper, you took me up to bed, heard my prayers, and then sat beside me until I dropped asleep.

You undoubtedly realize why I am recalling all these things . . . Some day soon God may send for you, to take you to a new home. Don't fear the summons, the strange journey, the dark messenger of death. At the end of the road you will find love and a welcome; you will be safe, there as here, in God's love and care. Surely he can be trusted to be as kind to you as you were years ago to me.

This is the final word and a fulfillment of the promise of his amazing grace. It is what we recall at the Easter season. It is what Easter is all about.

5

A Sure Hope

Most of us agree that the Sermon on the Mount is the greatest sermon in existence. As to the second greatest sermon, I would say it is the one of St. Paul in 1 Corinthians 15 and 16. He begins: "I declare unto you the gospel." That should be the purpose of any sermon.

The gospel is good news. It is the cure, but many sermons do not declare the gospel. Suppose I went to a physician and, after examination, he told me I had cancer. Then, suppose he set in to give me a history of cancer, telling me that cancer is a bad thing to have, that it destroys life, it brings great pain, eventually it will kill. All of that may be true but it would not be the good news. The gospel would be that there is a cure.

As a preacher I might tell people they are sinners, that sin destroys life, brings pain, and eventually sends one to hell. All of that may be true, but it is not the gospel.

Charles L. Allen, Senior Minister, First United Methodist Church, Houston, Texas.

The preacher that merely tells people how bad they are is missing his calling. We do not need to build a church to tell people of sin. We preach to tell people of the cure for sin. "I declare the gospel"—the good news, said St. Paul.

Then, in this sermon he tells us what the gospel is. *Christ died for our sins.* Unless we begin with the cross, we might as well not begin. There is only one cure for sin and that is the blood of Jesus Christ. Nothing else can cleanse a guilty soul.

Sin separates us from God, and, being separated from God, we are powerless to unite ourselves with God. Like the branch which is cut from the vine, we wither and die. Jesus, being God, has hold of the power of God. And because Christ became man, he is in reach of man. Thus, when by faith I take hold of the hand of Christ, I become united with God. Through Christ, God's power flows into me and gives me life.

A little girl came into the church and saw a cross on the altar. She said, "What is the plus sign doing on the table?" That is it. The cross is the plus between God and man. "The way of the cross leads home," we sing. That is the only way.

He rose again the third day. That is the second point of the gospel. If Christ had not risen, Paul points out five dreadful consequences: Our preaching is vain, our faith is vain, we are false witnesses, we are yet in our sins, and those who have fallen asleep in Christ are perished.

Take away the empty tomb and you destroy the Christian faith. The fact of his resurrection is the only assurance we have of eternal life. There are reasons why we might believe in life after death, but the resurrection of Christ changes mere hope into actual certainty.

Because he lives, we shall live also. We mortals become immortal. Why do we crowd our churches on Easter Sunday? We talk about the "Easter Parade," but it is not to show our new clothes. We go that Sunday especially because we long to have that assurance that we shall never die. "Death is swallowed up in victory," he said.

It is a fact that people attend church on Easter Sunday in much larger numbers than on any other day. Why is this?

Down deep in the heart of every person is a longing to know, to be sure of eternal life. A friend of Maud Royden once said, "Do not bother me now. Don't bother me never; I want to be dead, forever and ever." But that is not the feeling of very many. Most of us want to hear a word of certainty concerning life after death.

And on Easter Sunday we have the surest and most certain word that man possesses. In the long ago, Job asked, "If a man die, shall he live again?" (Job 14:14). And through the ages that question has been on the lips of humanity.

The Christian's answer to Job is the word of our Lord when he said, "Because I live; ye shall live also" (John 14:19). We place our whole faith in the fact of his resurrection from the dead. How sure can we be that he actually did rise? Let us examine the evidence.

To begin with Jesus was completely dead. There was a Jewish law that bodies could not remain on the cross on the Sabbath day. So they obtained permission from Pilate to break the legs of Christ and the two thieves and take them down. "But when they came to Jesus, and saw that He was dead already, they brake not his legs; but one of the soldiers with a spear pierced his side, and forthwith came there out blood and water" (John 19:31-34).

His body was wound in linen clothes, placed in a sepulchre which was hewn out of solid rock, and the door of the sepulchre was sealed with a large stone (Mark 15:42-47).

Certain people remembered that Jesus said he would rise, so they took especial precaution to see to it that no hoax was perpetrated. They, themselves, sealed the tomb and set a watch over it (Matt. 27:62-66).

Then there came a great earthquake. Those soldiers began to tremble and they fainted away (Matthew 28: 2-4). It was at this moment that Jesus rose from the tomb. Later the enemies of Christ bribed the soldiers to say that while they were asleep, his disciples came and stole his body (Matt. 28:11-15).

But look at that for a moment. First, it was a death penalty for a soldier to go to sleep on watch. And it is beyond belief that an entire company of soldiers would have done so. Also, the noise of moving the stone would surely have awakened some of them. Then, had that been the case, it would not have been necessary to bribe the soldiers to tell it.

It is possible for one to believe something so strongly that he thinks it happened even when it did not. But not one of Jesus' friends expected him to rise. On the way to the tomb the women were worrying about who would roll away the stone (Mark 16:3). Mary Magdalene ran to tell Simon Peter that they had taken the Lord out of the sepulchre (John 20:2). It did not occur to her he had risen.

That Sunday afternoon we see two of Jesus' friends walking back home to Emmaus. They were sad and hopeless (Luke 24:13-35). That same Sunday night his disciples assembled in an upper room, trembling with fear (John 20:19).

But many people were finally convinced that Jesus ac-

49

tually did rise. They saw him and heard him speak (John 20:11-31). They watched him eat actual food (Luke 24:41-43). Jesus invited one of them to feel his hands and side (John 20:27).

Later, one morning the disciples came in from fishing. They saw Christ on the shore, and when they got there, found that he had cooked breakfast for them (John 21:12-13). Finally, at least ten people saw him bodily leave the earth (Luke 24:50-51).

St. Paul talked to many who were with Christ and he tells us that Christ was seen of above 500 people at one time, that he was seen by Cephas, the twelve, James, and then all the apostles. And then Paul adds the supreme and undisputable proof, "He was seen of me also" (1 Cor. 15:5-8).

"He was seen of me." Today there are thousands who can give that same testimony. We sing: "He lives, He lives, Christ Jesus lives today . . . You ask me how I know He lives? He lives within my heart."

And on Easter we are surest.

The Easter After*

As You know,
It's the Easter after, Lord;
The dearest one to me
Is dead.
They said, "This is not so,
He's just gone on;
He loved His God,
And acted so;
You know he did.
Passed into
Another room;
Soon you'll find him,
For he is just away."

They say,
And say,
And say.

I nod,
And wish to You, God,
That they would stop,
And shout instead,
"Yes, yes, yes!
He is dead,
But death is swallowed
Up in victory.

*For sister Edith regarding her beloved Bert.

"No need for tears,
No need for fears,
For Jesus died
To open wide
The gates of heaven,
And death has lost its sting."

I hear You say,
"O bring your broken heart,
Your partedness,
Your sin
(It does come to that
Sometimes, Lord, I confess,
This separateness);
Enter in,
Loved child of mine,
For the Kingdom
That is to come
Is now;
Bow not to clock nor
Euphemism.
Why do you seek
The living among the dead?"

My beloved serves in Paradise today.
Risen!

As you said.

Sallie Chesham

6

A Why to Live for

Philippians 1:12–28a

In 1938, after a visit to the Holy Land, a certain minister dreamed a great dream. He wanted to erect a garden, a place of prayer, a chapel, in his home town of Covington, Kentucky. His hope was to bring the Holy Land to those who would never see it in person. And so land was purchased and flowers and trees were brought from twenty-four countries.

Many individuals contributed to the project. There was a carpenter's shop and tools from Nazareth. A replica of the open tomb was built. Overlooking the entire project was a gigantic statue of Christ which could be seen for miles. In 1959 he opened his beautiful dream park to the public, sort of a "religious Disneyland." It was called, appropriately enough, "The Garden of Hope." Almost immediately, however, the "Garden of Hope" ran into difficul-

Donald B. Strobe, Senior Minister, First United Methodist Church, Ann Arbor, Michigan.

ties. Most of the plants and trees, which were brought from around the world, died, for they could not endure the Kentucky climate. The garden did not have the visitors that were expected. Soon it went into bankruptcy. For twenty-one years the minister had planned and dreamed about his "Garden of Hope." But his dream failed. The park, I understand, is a sad and tragic sight today. Weeds have grown up everywhere. The chapel is padlocked, and the lonely statue of Christ has fallen into disrepair. The "Garden of Hope" is a failure.

It is a parable for us. The world seems to be running out of hope these days. Here we are, poised on the threshold of a future which seemed just a few short years ago to be pregnant with promise, but we find ourselves with the haunting fear that, as someone cynically put it, "the future is a thing of the past!" If nuclear warfare doesn't get us, then racial suicide will; and if, perchance, we should happen to survive both of those calamities, it is possible that we will suffocate in the smog of our own pollution. We have managed to put men on the moon, but the question now is: how much longer will there be men on the earth?

From nearly every quarter we hear pessimistic predictions. And the more expert a man is in his field, the more pessimistic he seems to be. Many feel that our world is running fresh out of "hope." Every thoroughfare seems to have a "No Exit" sign thrown across it. There just doesn't appear to be any hope left. The "Great Society" hasn't turned out to be so great after all. Our grandiose dreams and schemes have fallen flat. Thomas Howard, writer and professor, tells of the traumatic experience of shaking off the fundamentalist faith in which he was reared, and how difficult it was for him to come to a more mature understanding of life. He wrote a book about his experiences called *Christ the Tiger*, and while it ends on a note of hope, it contains these despairing words:

> Things have a way of falling to pieces. The shingles blow off the roof. The fender rusts through and the exhaust pipe drags. Cuffs fray, nylons run, hair falls out, joints stiffen, and wattles appear under our chin. Nothing is exempt . . . even our ideas.

It does seem that way at times, doesn't it? Some of us middleagers can remember a hit song of about twenty years ago titled "Life Gets Tedious, Don't It?" The singer, Carson Robison, complained about the well running dry and the cow doing the same; the food running out and the chickens stopping their laying. Then he laments, "And now I'm getting dandruff!" Trouble seems to come in bunches, like bananas. Right now our world appears to be up to its ears in trouble, and hope seems to be running out. Many people have come to a new appreciation of the old hymn which contains the words:

> Swift to its close ebbs out life's little day;
> Earth's joys grow dim; its glories pass away;
> Change and decay in all around I see . . .

That appears to be the order of the day.

There is a growing suspicion that life has lost its meaning, if it ever had any. This is what was really behind the so-called "Death of God Movement." The "death of God" means the death of meaning. Michael Harrington writes in *The Accidental Century*, "After God died, man who was supposed to replace Him, grew sick of himself. This resulted in a crisis of belief and disbelief, which made the twentieth century spiritually empty." We who live in the latter half of that twentieth century are the inheritors and victims of that prevailing mood of spiritual emptiness. Much of modern art, with its chaos and confusion, is trying to tell us this. The theatre reflects the same loss of meaning. Man is "Waiting for Godot," (which could mean "God") and Godot never comes. In most modern novels men and women are pushed here and there by an unknowing, uncaring fate and seem to be but helpless pawns on the chessboard of life. The novelist Saul Bellow speaks for many modern writers and playwrights when he says in *Herzog*:

> . . . what is the philosophy of this generation? Not God is dead, that period was passed long ago. Perhaps it should be stated death is God. This generation thinks— and this is its thought of thoughts—that nothing faithful, vulnerable, fragile can be durable or have any true power. Death waits for these things as a cement floor waits for a dropping light bulb.

But we don't have to turn to contemporary art or drama or literature to understand the meaninglessness of life. Many of us know from personal experience the pointless trivia which passes for "life" in too many of our lives. The psychiatrist Rollo May describes too many of us in *Man's Search for Himself:*

> The clearest picture of the empty life is the suburban man, who gets up at the same hour every weekday morning, takes the same train to work in the city, performs the same task at the office, lunches at the same place, leaves the same tip for the waitress each day, comes home on the same train each night, and has 2.3 children, . . . goes to church every Christmas and

Easter, and moves through a routine, mechanical existence year after year until he finally retires at sixty-five
and very soon thereafter dies of heart failure.

May adds, "I've always had the secret suspicion, however,
that he dies of boredom!" The real tragedy of it all is that,
although he "goes to church every Christmas and Easter,"
the man doesn't realize that the message which he hears
on those great days is supposed to transform his very existence!

*The biblical message of Christmas and Easter is that
there is hope . . . even in the midst of hopelessness; there
is life . . . even in the midst of death!* In the first century
deep darkness had settled upon the world. The religions
of the world seemed to be dying, or at least irrelevant and
ineffective. Military power and might ruled the nations.
Cruelty and evil were everywhere, and human life was
cheap. But then, on a Judean hillside, there came a message which has reverberated down the corridors of history with hope: "Fear not! For behold, I bring you good
tidings of great joy, which shall be to all the people! For
unto you is born this day in the city of David a Saviour,
which is Christ the Lord!" (Luke 2:10-11) With that great
message of hope the early Christian movement got its
start. And what high hopes those first disciples of Jesus
had! They thought that he would surely restore the kingdom to Israel! He would surely triumph over all of his
earthly foes and inaugurate a new era of peace and pros-
perity! But then . . . Jesus' life seemed to come to a
disastrous end. His enemies rose up against him, and put
him to death on trumped-up charges. He was "a disturber
of the peace," they said, an "upsetter of the status quo."
"He is dangerous!" his enemies shout over and over again

in the rock opera "Jesus Christ Superstar." And so they said, "Crucify him!" He was crucified, dead, and buried. And when that huge stone was rolled across the entrance to his tomb, a stone of grief and despair rolled across the hearts of the disciples. All of their hope and joy were gone. What else was there to live for? If life could treat someone as wonderful as Jesus with such cruelty . . . then what hope was there for lesser men?

But on the third day, when some women came to the tomb, they found the stone rolled away. And again came the message of hope: "Fear not! For I know that you seek Jesus of Nazareth who was crucified. He is not here; for he has risen, as he said!" (Matt. 28:5-6).

What actually happened that first Easter Sunday? I must confess that I don't know . . . but *something* did! The Gospel records are not clear about many of the details; and, indeed, some of the details seem to be contradictory. But they do proclaim one thing: there came a great transfusion of hope into a world dying of despair. Those defeated disciples were transformed from weaklings into witnesses. The fellowship which seemed to have been wiped out by the events of Good Friday suddenly burst upon the world after Easter Sunday with the glad, good news, "Christ is risen!" The minor miracle of that first Easter was the resurrection of the spirits of the disciples. They still knew that death was a solemn fact of life. But they also knew that beyond death there is life; death does not have the last word—God does! And that word is *Life!* They discovered that it is only when a man becomes unafraid to die, that he becomes unafraid to live. And live, they did! J. B. Phillips, in his little book, *New Testament Christianity,* gives us a fanciful picture of a senior angel instructing a junior angel about the meaning of Easter, and he says:

> They killed Him, all right, but He conquered death. The thing that most of them dread and fear all their lives, He broke and conquered. He rose again, and a few of them saw Him, and from then on became His utterly devoted slaves!

That infectious, contagious faith spread out into the world and spilled over into a man named Paul. When he wrote his letter to the Philippians, things were in a pretty sad state. He was in prison for his faith. His friends had deserted him, and his health was breaking down. The cause for which he had given his life seemed destined for defeat. A cruel and sadistic emperor was on the throne. Death was imminent. Yet that Philippian letter breathes an atmosphere of joy and hope. How come? The answer is found in Paul's succinct declaration of faith: "For me to live is Christ, and to die is gain!" (Phil. 1:21). J. B. Phillips translates this poignant passage:

> Living to me means simply "Christ," and if I died I should merely gain more of Him. I realize, of course, that the work which I have started may make it necessary for me to go on living in this world. I should find it very hard to make a choice. I am torn in two directions—on the one hand I long to leave this world and live with Christ, and that is obviously the best thing for me. Yet, on the other hand, it is probably more necessary for you that I should stay here on earth. That is why I feel pretty well convinced that I shall not leave this world yet, but shall be able to stand by you to help you forward in Christian living and to find increasing joy in your faith!

In spite of his difficulties, Paul's "Garden of Hope" had not dried up! He is saying that whatever happens, he cannot lose. If he should die in prison, that is okay, for it means that he will move into the nearer presence of Christ. If he should live, that is okay, too, for that means that he can continue to serve Christ here on earth. Either way, he cannot lose!

There is a story (perhaps apocryphal) which says that one day an eager woman came up to Ralph Waldo Emerson with the startling news that the world was coming to an end. Emerson is supposed to have replied, "That's all right. I can get along without it!" So could Paul. But can *we*? Just where does our ultimate allegiance and loyalty lie? Paul could make such startling statements because his life was wholeheartedly committed to Jesus Christ. He believed that his life was not in the hands of a blind, unreasoning fate but in the hands of a loving Father-God . . . a God who had revealed himself in the life, death, and resurrection of Jesus. Therefore, no harm could ultimately come to him. "For me to live is Christ, and to die is gain!" he said.

The German philosopher Nietzsche once said that "He who has a why to live for can put up with almost any how." What he meant, I think, is that one can endure almost anything if he believes that his experience has meaning beyond the present moment of pain or despair. His words, it seems to me, get to the root of the main spiritual problem that plagues our world today: the feeling that life has lost its meaning. We have never known so much nor possessed so much, yet never have we been so confused about the meaning of our human existence upon this earth. We need a recovery of hope, the kind of hope that sustained Paul in his trials: the faith that whatever happened to him, personally, nothing could happen to him, ultimately. "Hope," therefore, is a theological word. It does not refer to "wishful thinking," but from a Christian standpoint it means trust in the kind of God revealed in Jesus Christ. And I would suggest that the only hope that we have left is theological hope!

A recent cartoon depicts a jolly clergyman speaking to a parishioner, "What a heavenly day!" Then he stops and remarks, "But there I go, talking shop again!" But that is not too likely these days. We don't talk much about heaven anymore. Perhaps we are reacting against those people who are so "heavenly minded they are no earthly good," those who talk much about heaven and the here-after, but do little to help clean up the hells here on earth here and now. Perhaps we have been overly sensitive to the Marxist criticism that "religion is the opiate of the people," used to drug men's souls so that tyrants can en-slave their bodies. Too often in history it has worked out that way! But still, Christian hope is a basic part of our faith, and we neglect it to our own peril. For, as Nietzsche said, man can put up with almost anything if he feels that there is meaning and purpose behind it. But if he becomes convinced that life is only "a tale told by an idiot, full of sound and fury, signifying nothing . . ." then there is little hope for his life, and his joy quickly turns to ashes. In one of his books Leslie Weatherhead has written a good para-ble to describe the uses of hope:

> On a long sea journey round the world I once meditated on what would happen if the captain, one day, in the middle of the Pacific Ocean, summoned us all to the saloon and said something like this: "There is plenty of food on board. Life will proceed as before. Meals will be served, games played, dances arranged, concerts provided,

but I have decided not to make for a port. We shall just cruise round and round in the ocean until our fuel is exhausted and then I shall sink the ship."

Mark this. The next few days would *appear* just the same as those which preceded them. Only one thing would be different. The captain's speech would have snatched from every mind the concept of purpose, meaning and goal. And, in my opinion, very soon afterwards, on a dark night, first one and then another passenger would jump overboard. The mind hates meaninglessness.

Can it be, then, that the *why* of life is just as important as the *how?* Can it be that most of us have been asking the wrong questions? We want to know how to make a living, when the prior question is more important: how to make a *life*. In all our preoccupation with the question, "Will man survive?" have we forgotten to ask the more important questions, "What will man do if he does survive? What happens to him *ultimately?*" For, even under optimum conditions for human survival, our tenure on this planet is limited, at best. What then?

To this question the Christian faith answers, " 'Then' is " 'Eternal Life.' " But "Eternal Life," biblically speaking, is not merely an endless succession of time. Mere lengthening of time is not necessarily a good thing. George Bernard Shaw once remarked that he couldn't imagine anything worse than an eternity of George Bernard Shaw. But "Eternal Life" in the Bible does not refer to a quantity of life so much as to a quality of life, not so much to a *length* of life as to a *depth* of life. It refers to a depth and quality of life which have their beginnings in the here and now, and not merely in some future hereafter. "For me, to live is Christ!" said Paul. *Present* tense.

Whatever happens after death can safely be left in the hands of God. Sometimes people wonder whether or not a faith in the future life will cut the nerve of moral endeavor in this life. But I believe that a firm faith in the direction in which the world is traveling is a mighty fine thing to have to equip us for meeting the problems of the present. Christian hope means that life is open-ended. There are possibilities in every situation far beyond the mind of man to conceive. Nothing could have been bleaker than Paul's prospects when he wrote from prison; and yet he could write, "For me to live is Christ!"

In the latter years of his life, Robert Louis Stevenson struggled with tuberculosis. Yet he wrote letters of such good cheer from Samoa to his friends in Europe that they could hardly believe all that he was suffering. In one of his letters, he ends with these words: "I will not allow the medicine bottles on my mantelpiece to be the limits of my horizon!" Neither did Paul in a Roman prison. Nor did Dietrich Bonhoeffer in a German prison. His last words on this earth were a message to his friend Bishop Bell in England. "Tell him that for me this is the end, but also the beginning. With him I believe in the principle of our universal Christian brotherhood which rises above all national interests, and that our victory is certain!" Some time ago I attended a seminar at the seminary from which I graduated a number of years ago. During this seminar a professor of Old Testament from Germany was asked, "What is the task of the church in these despairing times?" He replied, "The same as it has always been: *to prepare men to die.*" At first I rejected that. What I am trying to do is to prepare men to *live.* But then I came to see that there is really no contradiction between the two.

To live well is to be prepared to die, for "Eternal Life" begins in the here and now, begins when one opens his heart to the eternal Christ.

The late Dr. J. Wallace Hamilton was one of the truly gifted and creative exponents of a relevant and biblical faith. In his book entitled *Horns and Haloes in Human Nature,* he told this story. It seems that during the First World War some church folks in London gave an entertainment for a company of soldiers who were on their way to the front. When it was over, the colonel asked a young officer who had the gift of ready speech to express the thanks of the men to the people. The young officer arose, and in some well-chosen words of wit and charm, expressed the soldiers' thanks to their hosts. And then, as if seeking some words with which to close, he said, "We're leaving now for France, the trenches, and maybe to die." He hadn't meant to say that. Looking around, he said, "Can anybody tell us how to die?" There was an awkward pause as though he had said the wrong thing, and a period of strained silence in which nobody said anything. Then someone walked quietly to the piano and began to sing the aria from "Elijah," "O Rest in the Lord." In the quiet that followed, as deep called unto deep, every man's soul was making its way back to some half-remembered thing to which he had always belonged.

Can anybody tell us how to die?
  Yes, *Christ* can.
    And also how to *live.*
      Thanks be to God.

7

To Jerusalem and Back

The old and the new live incongruously side by side in Jerusalem, which was the high point of the trip for most of the fifty-five Americans, Canadians, and Bermudeans who were pilgrim-travelers on a tour to the Middle East.

Darting in and out of old streets of Jerusalem are new American taxicabs, while in the very shadow of the city walls shepherds tend their flocks, still dressed much as they were two thousand years ago.

During our five days in Jerusalem we were housed in two hotels which somehow symbolize these contrasts. One, the American Colony, is a converted harem in the middle of the city. The hostess, Mrs. Vester, is an expatriate American. The other, the Palace Hotel, is a glass and steel structure on the Mount of Olives, with a startling view of the city topped by the beautiful mosque, the Dome of the Rock. Sami Sawalha, a Jordanian with a

Bruce Larson, President, Faith at Work.

master's degree from the University of Michigan, and his lovely American wife, were perfect hosts.

To every pilgrim who goes to the Holy Land his own trip is unique—though thousands of others have journeyed before him—and ours was to us quite special. At almost every point along the way God gave us experiences that crystallized for an unforgettable moment the significance of the holy places in the life of Jesus.

Close to Bethlehem are the Shepherds' Fields where traditionally the angels made their announcement on that first Christmas Eve. As we sang Christmas carols gathered in a cave in the hillside, we understood what Jesus meant when he said he was "the door of the sheep." There is a narrow passageway in the front of the cave, the only way for an animal or man to enter or leave. If a shepherd sleeps there, truly he is a door.

Another day we spent a memorable hour in the Church of the Paternoster, the traditional place where Jesus taught his disciples the Lord's Prayer, and where today the Lord's Prayer is carved in stone in scores of languages. As we gathered there, it was thrilling to hear individuals in our group pray in more than twenty languages, including Greek, Latin, and Russian, and finally to be led in prayer by Connie Elmes, a pastor to the deaf in Chicago, in the universal sign language.

One morning my wife, Hazel, and I with Ray Nash, a physician from Bermuda, headed for the Dome of the Rock, a mosque of exceeding beauty and great significance to all Moslems. The mosque is built on the site of Solomon's temple, which is also the traditional site of Abraham's sacrifices. One of the walls surrounding the courtyard incorporates a bit of the old temple wall, the historic "wailing wall" for the Jews, where traditionally they gathered to wail and lament the lost glories of Israel.

The Dome of the Rock mosque is one of the three most holy places of the Moslem world. To be a true hadji (pilgrim), able to wear a special hat (much like a fez with a turban around the base), one must visit all three: Mecca, Medina, and Jerusalem.

This exquisite building with its golden dome is one of the truly beautiful sights of the city, but our recollection of the doorkeeper at the entrance to the mosque is even more vivid. A huge man, he wore an English coat and vest and the kind of skirt so common in the Arab world, topped by the traditional hat of the hadji. He sat barefooted and crosslegged, fondling his "worry beads" and making appreciative comments on all the American women who went in and out of the mosque.

We had opportunities, two by two, to visit in private homes. Charles and Betty Cleland, who are both physicians, accidentally discovered the only physician practicing within the old walled city and spent a wonderful afternoon in his home. Many in our party made chance acquaintances like this and got to know some of the people of Jerusalem personally.

One rainy afternoon Lloyd Ogilvie and I took a cab to Bethany where Mary and Martha once lived and where Lazarus was raised from the dead, then we walked the two miles back to Jerusalem, not along the main road, but over the hills in the way Jesus must often have walked to Jerusalem. The landscape and much of the architecture seemed ancient. Children came out to greet us as they must have greeted Jesus. Lloyd was wearing a Scottish tam and I a "Professor Henry Higgins hat," so we were a source of interest and amusement to young and old alike along the way.

Midway we stopped at Bethphage where Jesus began his triumphal entry. A friendly peg-legged doorkeeper let us into a little walled Roman Catholic church. We were alone for some time, and such poignant thoughts came. I thought how often Jesus had told people to say nothing of his healings or miracles. Then at one particular moment in time it seemed right to offer himself and his ministry to the world. We were in the place of that turning point in Jesus' strategy, and we sensed how our Lord had to walk by faith.

It came to us how important it is for every Christian to do God's work in God's time so as not to wonder, Have I missed it? Was it last year? Is it next year? Is this the time?

We continued our walk and finally, over a hill, Jerusalem lay before us. A small plaque on a mud wall confirmed that this was the place where Jesus wept over the city.

Along our walk we had been joined by several young boys. We played ball with them and conversed as best we could. Suddenly the boys asked if they could get us some girls. In that moment we realized how little the world has changed since the day that Jesus stood where we stood and wept over this beautiful, glorious old city. Jesus' love and offer of himself is as relevant now as it was then in the face of man's need and loneliness.

As we started down the hill into the valley, we passed the Garden of Gethsemane. The day before our entire group had visited the Garden for one of the most moving experiences I can remember. Many of the olive trees are very old and must have been standing when our Lord prayed here alone. In this walled spot, full of flowers and trees, we walked and prayed and wept openly. Just before

68

we left we gathered in one corner, read the account of Jesus' prayer in Gethsemane, and sang a hymn.

One cloudy, overcast afternoon we walked along the Via Dolorosa, Jesus' route to the cross. Though the pavement of the old city of Jerusalem is now many feet below the present one, the whole atmosphere seems much as it must actually have been on that first Good Friday. I sensed a timelessness about this street.

A huge sign over one shop said, in English, "Souvenirs of the Via Dolorosa." How ironic! Jesus sought to overthrow the commercialization of religion. Now the destroyer of commercialism has been commercialized.

At the end of the Via Dolorosa is the Church of the Holy Sepulchre, an ornate but gloomy structure, the traditional place where our Lord's body lay in the tomb. The church is in great need of repair, but so many Christian groups have a vested interest in it that they cannot agree on any course of action. And so, at what is supposed to be the holiest of all places, we find a dramatic reminder of the divisions in the Body of Christ!

As I sat resting in the courtyard of this church, I saw a burly policeman solemnly standing guard at the door. A small boy came up and began to maul him, pull at his belt, and play with his gun. The policeman said nothing in the face of this affectionate indignity. A stranger nearby noticed my amazement and whispered, "His son!" I nodded knowingly and smiled. My new friend added, "His only son," and then these final words, "from two wives."

How few words it sometimes takes to communicate! These brief words gave me a whole story. And how apropos it was to the place in which we were standing where long ago God gave his son—his only son!

There is another, more recent, site that archaeologists have suggested may be the tomb of our Lord. It is called Gordon's Garden Tomb, discovered by General Gordon, an amateur archaeologist. It is beautiful, quiet, and unspoiled and is hewn out of a huge rock on the hillside.

We were responsible for Sunday morning services there and were joined by a large group of Presbyterians from Oklahoma. Rain fell during the services and we sensed something of the sadness of Jesus' death, then, as the sun broke through, something of the joy of the resurrection, which transcends geography and time as the most amazing fact in history.

After visiting Jerusalem, the Sea of Galilee, Nazareth, and Haifa, our group had a final time together in Caesarea on the shores of the Mediterranean Sea. The sun was setting and the wind was up, the Mediterranean dark and glistening.

The fifty-five of us gathered in the shadows of an old Roman aqueduct. There were tears of sadness at the imminent farewell. There were prayers and hymns and finally the apostolic benediction. Like the early Christians, we had been in the holy city with our Lord, and now we were scattering to "the uttermost parts" to serve him and to carry to others the good news of his life and resurrection.

8

There's Nothing to Fear

Mark 16:6

It is virtually impossible for us to feel the total despair which gripped the disciples after Jesus had gasped his last breath on the cross. The One for whom they had left friends and fortune, the One who had come to them with freshness and authenticity, the One who lived and taught as no one else was now taken from them, a lifeless corpse on a criminal's cross. The amazing drama of this One they had called Master and Messiah had ended all too abruptly on that dismal Friday afternoon.

For three years they had followed him wherever he went. They had traversed the dusty lanes of Palestine, never ceasing to be amazed at his words and deeds. How could they ever forget what they had seen and heard?

They had heard him teach, "as no other man had taught." His teaching had a ring of truth and authority which was lacking in that of most religious leaders of the

Gary W. Demarest, Senior Minister, La Canada Presbyterian Church.

day. He taught with simple clarity. And they would never forget the many parables that he had told, simple stories from nature and everyday life with profound spiritual and practical meaning.

The major theme of Jesus' teaching had focused upon the Kingdom of God—a concept of the rule and reign of God in human life. They had long harbored ideas, shaped by their own understanding of the Scriptures, as to what the Kingdom of God would be like and how it would come in Messianic fulfillment. But so much of his teaching had cut squarely across their established beliefs that it was difficult for them to break out of their molds and respond to him in faith. Yet what he taught about the Kingdom of God struck a responsive note in their hearts again and again, and for the first time the Scriptures and history and reality began to fit together.

Unlike some of the political and ecclesiastical concepts of the Kingdom which they had held, he taught about a Kingdom of love, a Kingdom in which God's love opened the way to new relationships with him and with one another.

Could they ever forget the story of the prodigal son and the elder brother? Could it really be that God loves his rebellious children so much that he really is waiting eagerly for their return? Could it be that God is a party-giving God who pulls out all the stops to celebrate the return of his rebel son?

The more they listened to Jesus teach, the more credible he became. Not because he told them what they wanted to hear, but because what he told them corresponded with reality and with life. It was as though he had given God a new face, a face of love and mercy. And yet it wasn't a new face at all. It had been there all along.

They just hadn't seen God that way until Jesus made it clear.

It wasn't just his teaching which had drawn their commitment and loyalty, rather it was his whole style of life which authenticated the teaching. They had watched him when he was fresh and when he was tired and when he was under great pressure from hostile crowds. They had even watched him when he was betrayed by friends. At every point, his life demonstrated what he taught.

They were amazed again and again at his demonstration of love to the losers and the outcast. Far from catering to the powerful and the wealthy, he embodied all of the precepts of the ancient prophets in his commitment to justice and righteousness for all men. And it had become clear to them that he was headed for a devastating confrontation with the religious and political leaders of his day.

Moved by his teaching, given courage by his life, finding in him a basis for hope and love, they had responded to his demands and had left everything to follow him. Jesus had never promised an easy way. But it was precisely in the context of costly commitment that they had found their greatest joy in being his disciples. They had pinned their highest hopes and their deepest aspirations on him.

And then it happened!

With dizzying speed, in less than a week, their whole world caved in! It hadn't really occurred to them that the confrontation they had anticipated would end up with Jesus on a cross.

What do you do when all of your dreams have been shattered? Where do you turn when your whole basis for hope has been denied? Can you really believe in a God of love and justice when you see Jesus hanging on a cross? These were the questions that haunted them as they huddled together in a locked room on that terrifying weekend.

Join them in your imagination if you can. Wait with them there, and share their fears and their confusion. At any minute they may hear the tramp of the soldiers' boots, the pause at the door, the forceful knock, and the word from the soldier, "You're next!"

But the soldiers didn't come. They weren't pursued and dragged off to crucifixions—at least not yet. Instead of soldiers there came unbelievable reports. Some women came with what may have seemed to be hallucinatory reports that they had seen him alive in the garden near the place of his burial. If this could have been passed off as such, it was no longer so after Peter and John had returned from their inspection of the tomb. They had found it empty, just as the women had said. Moreover, they had found the graveclothes—the linen cloth used to wrap a body for burial—lying in the very configuration of his body. Then came the report from the disciples who had just returned from that strange journey to Emmaus. They insisted that they had been with none other than the risen Lord himself.

In spite of the reports, it was still not possible for them to accept the fact of his resurrection from the dead. The magnitude of the fear that gripped them overshadowed the possibility of their ready acceptance of the good news.

Fear has that way of stifling faith, doesn't it? We can become so convinced of the power of evil that we really have difficulty accepting the transcendence of the good.

It is at this point that the importance of the resurrection of Jesus *as historical reality* becomes essential. For

74

me, the most convincing evidence of the resurrection of Jesus from the dead lies not in the initial reports of the witnesses but in the remarkable transformation of that frightened group of defeated disciples into a band of courageous and dynamic witnesses and martyrs.

The resurrection of Jesus was no mere philosophy of immortality dreamed up by terrified people hiding behind locked doors. Mere memory of a great teacher who died for a cause cannot in itself account for the changes experienced by that motley crew. To me, the power of the resurrection is best seen in the context of the terrifying fear known by the disciples after Jesus' death.

The fear that they experienced after the crucifixion is not unlike the fear experienced by men in every generation who are confronted with the ultimate issues of good and evil. To live is to know fear about the future. There has never been a time, and there will never be a time, when the ultimate triumph of good over evil, of love over hate, can be assumed or demonstrated from the raw data of history. It always seems as though there is nothing but doom ahead. An editorial entitled, "Has the Future Ever Looked Darker?" put it this way:

> It is a gloomy moment in history. Not in the lifetime of any man who reads this paper has there ever been so much grave and deep apprehension. Never has the future seemed so dark and incalculable. In France, the political cauldron seethes and bubbles with uncertainty. England and the British Empire are being sorely tried and exhausted in a social and economic struggle. The United States is beset with racial, industrial, and commercial chaos, drifting we know not where. Russia hangs like a storm cloud on the horizon of Europe . . . menacing and foreboding.

The editorial appeared in *Harper's Magazine* in 1847. However, this in no way minimizes the severity and the urgency of the problems of our generation. But it does help us to gain much needed perspective as to our place in history. To be alive in any age is to know and share the reality of fear and anxiety about the future. This was where the disciples were on that dark and perplexing weekend long ago. It is where we are today.

Only what changed the disciples of Jesus can transform us today. What set them free from their defeat and despair was nothing other than the reality of the resurrection of Jesus from the dead. That Jesus had conquered death was the basis of a new hope and joy. The central message of the resurrection is clearly stated in our text: "Fear nothing, he has risen!"

It is important to note that the resurrection did not change the world in which the disciples lived, but it did change *them*, dramatically and drastically. It was the risen Christ who changed them, and it is the same risen Christ who can change us!

The disciples moved out from behind their locked doors into a world that was the same. It was still a frightening world. Rome was still Rome. The political and military structures and powers went about their business as usual, taking little if any notice of this event that was to transform the disciples and set in motion a movement that would completely outlive the seemingly eternal glories of Rome.

The religious leaders of the day took notice of the resurrection but only proceeded to find means of explaining it away. Failing in this, they took further measures to stifle the reports and later to stamp out the movement that had its birth in the empty tomb.

The world of human relationships continued to have its ups and downs. Even Peter and Paul within the early Christian community had some sharp differences that were never fully reconciled. Conflict between parents and children, husbands and wives, friends and associates, was still very much a part of their lives. Failure and defeat were still with them. The ultimate sign of human failure, death itself, was still a reality even to those who had encountered the triumph of Jesus over death.

Sin continued to show its deadly power all around them. In spite of all that Jesus had been and done, in spite of the resurrection, sin remained the same destructive and disruptive reality in human life.

We mustn't lose sight of this simple fact that the world to which they returned after they had been liberated by the power of Christ's resurrection was the same old world it had always been. Only *they* were different!

In the light of the resurrection, they could face all of the realities of the world in confidence and with courage. They could know that there was nothing to fear, for all of the forces of evil could not kill Christ! The victory over sin and death was won. And the message came to them— even as it comes to us, *"Fear nothing, He has risen!"*

The message of Easter begins with the historical reality of the resurrection of Jesus from the dead. The fact of the resurrection is the cornerstone of the Christian faith. It stands for all time as the certitude that God is alive and present in this world—the assurance of the ultimate triumph of love and justice in God's time.

The reality of the resurrection can become the dynamic of a creative and meaningful style of life for you and me. Living in the light of the resurrection gives us *a new freedom*. Since Christ has conquered the last enemy—death itself—we can throw ourselves into the struggle for love and justice with abandon and become, as the Japanese Christian Kagawa was fond of saying, "God's gamblers." Knowing that the victory has been won, we are set free, even to fail. We can handle the loss of some of the battles when we know that the war has been won.

Living in the light of the resurrection gives us *a new perspective*. We need not be afraid of the evil around us nor give in to despair about the present or the future. Recently a friend of mine was asked this question, "Do you feel optimistic about the future?" "No," he replied, "I don't feel optimistic about the future, but I am filled with hope."

Christian perspective sees the future in the light of the resurrection and is grounded in hope. Hope is based upon reality, not upon appearance. Even when things appear to be at their worst, the resurrection reality gives us the basis for hope.

Place your trust in the risen Christ who was dead but is now alive. Move out into the world. It will not have changed, but you will! Let the crucified and risen Christ send you out into his world with a new courage and a new perspective and a new hope, knowing that he has risen—*there's nothing to fear!*

9

Trying to Stop
the Inevitable

Have you ever tried to stop the inevitable? Twice in my life I tried to stop what was almost inevitable. The first time I was a school boy, playing catcher on a baseball team. The batter tipped the ball. I missed it with my glove, and my nose tried to stop the ball. A bit later, when I was in high school, I tried to block a punt with my nose. When your nose tries to stop a ball, it is the nose that gets crushed. I read not long ago about wealthy New York bankers trying to stop the depression of the early thirties by buying stocks. You get yourself crushed by trying to stop the inevitable.

This was the condition of Pilate and those around him. They had crucified our Lord. He was dead. He had said he was going to rise again. They rolled a great stone up against the door of the tomb. They secured it with the

---

Thomas A. Fry, Co-pastor, Second Presbyterian Church, Memphis, Tennessee.

Roman seal and put guards there. Can you imagine the God who took the sun in his hand and flung it into the sky being thwarted by a stone pushed in front of a tomb? Can you imagine the God who created the nucleus of the atom being thwarted by a contingent of soldiers with swords? You can make the tomb secure, but once God is on the march you just do not stop him.

One of the problems of our generation is that we are frustrated. Our plans seem to go awry. We can't sleep. We can't adjust ourselves. Fighting against God is about to destroy us. Perhaps this is the reason we spend hundreds of millions of dollars a year in our country on synthetic peace. In 1969 there were approximately 37,273,-000,000 aspirins bought, and approximately 1,542,000,000 sleeping pills were used. We are frustrated trying to fight the inevitable, trying to fight the will of God. This was the case with Pilate.

What could be more frustrating than trying to stop God's plan to raise Jesus from the dead? Compare the plight of these individuals with the joy of those who could sing,

> Mine eyes have seen the glory of the coming of the Lord.
>> He is tramping out the vintage where the grapes of wrath are stored.
> He hath loosed the fearful lightning of his terrible swift sword.
>> His truth is marching on.
>
> He is sounding forth his trumpet which shall never call retreat.
>> He is sifting out the hearts of men before his judgment seat.
> Oh be swift, my soul, to answer him, be jubilant my feet.
>> His truth is marching on.

When God marches, little stones, Roman guards, and the best laid plans of mice and men are of no avail.

This raises for me the question of God's overall plan for my life, now and eternally.

Jesus clearly indicates that this life is a preparation for the life to come.

This life is but the first inch of the yardstick. This is but the grapefruit league ballgame that comes before the major league season begins. This is the grammar school before you move into high school. This is but the fetal stage of life, and death marks the beginning of the fullness of life.

Is there any proof of these affirmations? I could recite many so-called proofs, but I'd have to admit that they are intimations of the immortality of man rather than proofs of immortality. It is strange that some folk think you should believe anything that seems to be a proof of something that you want. Wishful thinking thus becomes a substitute for integrity. I think that we should be just as careful to examine proofs of what we believe, as we are to examine proofs of what we do not believe. There's only one thing that convinces me there is something beyond the grave, and that is the fact that Jesus Christ rose from the grave. He rose and said that we would rise, and I am convinced that he knows what he is talking about.

What indications do we have that Jesus rose?

This brings up another question. What indication do we have that Jesus actually rose from the grave? What kind of proof can we accept for an historic event? We cannot be there to see history reenacted. How do you prove that the North won the battle of Gettysburg? How do you prove that the British won at Waterloo? We don't

81

have any records or film. We really don't have a report from Walter Cronkite, Frank McGee, or Harry Reasoner on Gettysburg or Waterloo. How do we know these ever happened? Let's take the first World War. How do we know that England, France, and the United States were on the winning side?

There are two ways we know. First of all, we know some people who participated in the events described. We know soldiers who were in the Battle of the Marne, and who were party to the signing of the Treaty of Versailles. But there is a second way. We know no one who was at Gettysburg. All participants are dead. We know that the North beat the South at Gettysburg because in 1862 we had two countries and now we have one. If the South had won at Gettysburg, we would have had a Confederate States of America and a United States of America. If the South had won, the southern troops would have marched on to Washington. We have one united government now rather than two. The events of subsequent history are adequate proof that the North won the Battle of Gettysburg.

I think we have to use the same type of proof about the resurrection of our Lord. How do we know it happened? Paul says, "I delivered to you as of first importance what I also received, that Christ died for our sins in accordance with the scriptures, that he was buried, that he was raised on the third day in accordance with the scriptures, and that he appeared to Cephas, then to the twelve. Then he appeared to more than five hundred brethren at one time, most of whom are still alive, though some have fallen asleep. Then he appeared to James, then to all the apostles. Last of all, as to one untimely born, he appeared also to me" (1 Cor. 15:3-9). Thus we have the record of witnesses.

Also you can prove an historic event by its effect on history. The fact that within thirty or forty years a small group from in and around Jerusalem had completely turned history upside down and had changed the whole course of the Roman empire indicates that something significant happened. When you read the early documents, all indications are that Jesus rose from the dead. Death is but the open door to something bigger than we are and have.

We believe that death is this open door to joy and judgment

It is as difficult for us to know what life beyond the grave is like as for a fetus inside its mother's womb to describe the meaning of adult human life.

Jesus gave three pictures that have helped me.

He says that death is like a wedding. Weddings are not fulfillment but commencement. While they mark the end of an era, they are significant because they mark the beginning of a newer, more important era. So death is like a wedding.

Death is also described as being like a feast or banquet. A banquet is a time of levity and enjoyment. So death is to be interpreted as the beginning of a period of joy.

Death is further described as being like going home. If I drove home in the afternoon in the same spirit that many organists play "Going Home" at a funeral, I question if I would be very welcome. For most of us who work, going home is a thing greatly to be desired, anxiously awaited. While we like our work, the statement "Let's go home" is usually welcomed.

Some have suggested that going home is a matter of peace. It may be for some people, but it has never been so with me. Home is where I have responsibilities and things that need to be done. Home is where people count on me, and so I interpret death in the light of this concept of going home.

I recall graduation at Davidson College. We received our invitations a number of months in advance. One boy sent out over one hundred invitations. We finished exams about four days before graduation. The day after exams were over, this friend of mine received a notice to come to the dean's office. He had flunked two courses. The boy admitted to the dean that he had not studied. He had just loafed the last semester. They decided to give him a reexam in both courses. He took the reexams the next day after having spent the afternoon, the evening, and all night studying. He flunked them again. They had a special meeting of the full faculty there at Davidson, and the faculty did a most unusual thing. They decided that starting at five o'clock the morning of graduation, they would give this boy another set of reexams. So at five o'clock he had one reexam, and at eight o'clock he had the other. He flunked them both. His family was there, but the boy did not graduate. You cannot blame his failure on the faculty. The boy just had not prepared himself. Just as you cannot blame the college for the boy's failure, so I do not think you can blame God for man's failure.

This is the meaning of the parable of the sheep and goats. Some go to the right. Some go to the left. This is the meaning of many of Jesus' parables about death. Death is the entrance into joy, but for those who are not prepared, it is the entrance into judgment. This life we have now is but a preparation for a greater life. Death itself is the great wedding feast, or is, to use another illustration, the great commencement service for true life.

84

What happens when Christians die?

What happens beyond this commencement service? What happens beyond this wedding feast? We do not know, but we do have certain indications.

1. New responsibility. For example, we are sure that beyond this life a new responsibility is given to each one of us. Death is not the gateway into indolence. It is a promotion. It is not retirement. It is the acceptance of a more important job. Never think that death means partial or total retirement. It is the acceptance of new responsibilities. In the parable of the talents the man who had five talents made five more and the Lord said, "Well done, good and faithful servant. Thou hast been faithful in a few things. I will make thee ruler over many things." He does not say that you are going to be sent out to a South sea island to retire. Rather we are to be made ruler over many things.

2. Reunion. It is a place of reunion. When David's son died, he said, "Surely I shall go to be with him." Do you recall singing, "Friends will be there I have loved long ago?" An old Scotsman, when asked if he would know people in heaven, replied, "Do you think I'll have less sense there than now?" Our brains will be expanded. We see things through a glass darkly, but then face to face.

3. Reward. It is also a place of reward. "Well done. Thou hast been faithful in little. I will make thee ruler over much." "Lay not up for yourselves treasures on earth where moth and rust doth corrupt, but lay up treasures in heaven."

I recall Mr. R. F. Dillard of Blackstone, Virginia. He had been an elder in that church for seventy years. Once he said to me, "Tom, I want to die." I was shocked and asked, "Why, Mr. Dillard?" He said, "Well, you see, none of my contemporaries are left. My wife and my loved ones have gone on, and I want to be reunited with them. My Lord is there." He then added, "As you know, Tom, I have made more money than any man in this area. I've been a wealthy man, but I've tried to give it all to the Lord and to the church, and all my treasure is there. I don't have any money. I've laid my treasure over there, and I want to go and be with my friends and my loved ones, my work." Lay not up for yourselves treasures on earth. Lay up treasures in heaven.

4. A place of rejoicing. It is also a place of rejoicing. It will be like a commencement service. There are a lot of tears at a wedding and at a graduation service. There are tears as the family wonders how their son ever made it. There are tears on the part of the mothers, because they realize that their child is leaving home. There is joy at a commencement or a wedding, but there are also tears.

How can we be saved? "God so loved the world that he gave his only begotten Son, that whosoever believeth on him should not perish but have everlasting life." It is only through faith in Christ that we can enjoy this place we call paradise or heaven.

Pilate, who knew nothing about death, was completely frustrated because he tried to fight against God. He thought he could stop anybody from getting into or out of the tomb with a guard of Roman soldiers, a Roman seal, and a great stone. When our eyes see the glory of the coming of the Lord, we realize that a man cannot fight against him.

It is the Easter season. Are you frustrated? Do you

sense a hopelessness in life? Have you put yourself on one side and let God be on the other? You've used the right words. But is it real personal acceptance? Have you accepted his will, his salvation, or have you been standing off trying to seal against his way with a little Roman seal or sword or stone?

10

The Price Love Paid

Galatians 6:14

What a strange exclamation that is! Why boast about
the cross on which a young Jew was executed? As they
read Paul's impassioned outburst, no wonder people wrin-
kle their brows in bafflement. Nobody in his right mind
composes hymns extolling the hangman's noose or sports a
replica of the guillotine or decorates a church steeple with
a model of Sing Sing's electric chair. Why, then, glory in
the cross, that ghastly symbol of cruelty, shame, and
death?

Years ago when Christianity was first propagated in
China, a native editor, antagonistic to the gospel, mock-
ingly inquired: "Why should the followers of Jesus reverence the instrument of his punishment and consider it so
to represent him as not to venture to tread upon it? Would
it be commonsense, if the father or ancestor of a house

Vernon C. Grounds, President, Conservative Baptist Theological
Seminary, Denver, Colorado.

had been killed by a shot from a gun or a wound from a sword, that his sons and grandsons should reverence the gun or sword as if it were their father or ancestor?" That is a question which cries out for a satisfactory answer. Why do Christians glory in the cross?

We do so for one overwhelming reason. To us the cross of Calvary is the time-abiding, heart-assuring, all-sufficient revelation of God's love. In the words of 1 John 3:16: "Hereby perceive we the love of God, because he laid down his life for us, and we ought to lay down our lives for the brethren." That, in brief, is why we glory in the bloody gibbet on which a young Jew was done to death. For that young Jew was really God incarnate laying down his life for us in a love which eludes the grasp of human thought.

Perhaps we do not realize that apart from Calvary there is simply no convincing evidence to support the New Testament credo, "God is love." In nature, for example, we find no support for that central tenet of our faith, the love of God. Whether we study snowflakes under a microscope or survey the midnight heavens from the Mount Wilson observatory—no matter what scientific instruments or techniques we may use—the verdict is the same. Nowhere in nature do we find convincing evidence to substantiate the proposition that God is love.

In nature, admittedly, we find convincing evidence that Intelligence and Wisdom and Power must be the Ground of our universe. In fact, we find evidence enough to conclude that our cosmos probably owes its existence to a Creator, and a personal Creator at that, a Person of limitless power and intelligence. But nowhere do we find any convincing evidence that the Creator of the universe is a holy Father of infinite love. Of course there is the beauty

89

of roses, and we all admire roses. There is the haunting melody of the wood thrush as it sings at dusk, and we all enjoy that plaintive sound. There is the magnificence of dawn over the mountains, and we all thrill to watch the light beat back the darkness. Yet none of this proves that the Creator of the universe is necessarily a holy Father of love. Why not?

Imagine a Minnesota valley in autumn, apparently peaceful, tranquil and calm. In reality, however, that edenic scene is a battlefield. For in that rainbow-hued valley men are killing foxes, foxes are killing hawks, hawks are killing sparrows, sparrows are killing worms, and worms are eating men who once killed foxes. And we say glibly that God is love! Do we find the love of God revealed in the fangs of a rattlesnake? God is love! Do we find the love of God revealed in the lashing fury of a tornado? God is love! Do we find the love of God revealed in the lightning which electrocutes its victim? God is love! Do we find the love of God revealed in the avalanche of snow which snuffs out the lives of travelers driving through a mountain pass? God is love! Do we find the love of God revealed in the flood which drowns a city? God is love! Do we find the love of God revealed in the grain fungus which causes multitudes of people in India to die of starvation? God is love! We believe that, to be sure. Faith in a Father of grace and mercy lies at the very heart of Christianity. But where in nature do we find any convincing evidence to substantiate that central conviction?

Nor when we turn from nature to history do we find any convincing evidence to support the New Testament credo that "God is love." Do we find God's love revealed in the sadistic orgies of a Nero? Do we find God's love revealed in the tortures of the Spanish inquisition? Do we find God's love revealed in the Nazi gas chambers where millions of Jews perished for the unspeakable crime of not being born Gentile? Do we find God's love revealed in the concentration camps of Soviet Russia, the most monstrous system of slave labor that the world has ever seen? Do we find God's love revealed in the bomb that atomized Hiroshima? Do we find God's love revealed in all the injustice and frustration and heartbreak which constitutes the fabric of history?

God is love! What a Pollyanna creed that is! Go and preach that creed to a young woman with a baby in her arms as she holds a crumpled telegram in her hands, announcing that her husband has been killed in battle. God is love! Go and preach that creed to the victims of flood and famine in East Pakistan. God is love! Go and preach that creed to the Arab refugees in the Middle East. God is love! Where do we find any convincing evidence in nature or history to substantiate that thesis which we so glibly take for granted? Let us confess the truth: convincing evidence seemingly cannot be discovered. Maybe that is why an H. G. Wells character exclaims, "I don't believe there's a God Who is responsible for all of mankind's woes. But if there is a God, I'm not going to bow before him. I'm going to spit in his face!" That is undiluted blasphemy, of course, yet we can appreciate the genesis of such blasphemy. The ugly facts of existence apparently negate the idea that the Power Which sustains our universe is an infinite Person with a heart of holy love.

Then why do we Christians still cling to our credo? Why do we still believe and stoutly assert that God is love? Are we just plain stupid? Are we intellectually asleep? Are we blind to the tragic realities of existence?

Or if we cannot plead stupidity, are we downright dis-honest? Perhaps we realize how tragic life is but refuse to admit it. Or are we spineless cowards, afraid to look the horrendous realities full in the face, and therefore clinging in self-deception to the illusion that God is love? Why is it, anyway, that we keep on repeating our creed? We believe it not because we are necessarily ignorant or dishonest or spineless. We believe it because we take into account one world-transforming fact unbelief ignores. And that is the fact of Calvary! It is that shining and decisive fact which throws a flood of light upon the darkness of nature and history, persuading us that there really is a loving God.

The cross on which Jesus Christ died convinces us of at least three things. First, it assures us that God is not responsible for the evils from which humanity is suffering. Suffering is in the world. But it is not here because God foreordained it. No, indeed! Calvary's cross reveals that suffering is here because of human sin, and hence man's suffering is ultimately self-inflicted. Second, the cross assures us that in fathomless love God is throwing all of his resources into battle against the evils which blight our experience. Third, the cross assures us that in the fullness of time God will change life's tragedies into glorious victory.

This, then, is the ultimate meaning of the cross. The Creator of the universe, the Source of all existence, the Ground of being in its totality—not because of some external pressure, not because of some cosmic necessity, not because of some inescapable fate—was willing to perish in anguish and ignominy upon the cross for just one reason: He loved us! God was not forced to die by some external pressure. He was not the victim of some cosmic necessity.

God was not under the compulsion of some inescapable fate. Nothing of the sort! God died because He loved us!

When we are confronted with the cross, we come face to face with mysteries which are entirely beyond our searching out. But what glimpses of its meaning we can catch assure us that, in spite of all the contrary evidence, God is really limitless love.

Consider, if it does not strike you as a rash venture in human presumption, the cost of Calvary. What did Calvary cost God the Son?

It cost him agony of body. And to appreciate that agony, we watch our Lord in Gethsemane as he prays alone beneath the trees until he breaks out in a bloody sweat. We see him as he is betrayed with a treacherous kiss and is hurried about sleeplessly all through the hours of the night. We watch him as he is brutally flogged, and weary and exhausted, he is compelled to carry his cross through the streets of Jerusalem toward Golgotha. We watch our Lord as he is dragged to the hilltop where calloused Roman legionnaires drive spikes through his hands and feet. Men, remember, are killing their God! We watch him as there in the sun our Lord hangs in naked shame and, quivering in anguish, dies for us. Why is he suffering like that? Love alone is the answer.

God the Son suffered more, however, than agony of body. He suffered agony of heart as well. We know that he had blessed the mutitudes. Yet as he hung there on the cross, they cursed him. He had wept over Jerusalem, yet on the cross he was laughed to scorn by the very people over whom he had wept. Although many times the Lord had his hands in healing benediction upon diseased bodies, yet on the cross his holy hands were stretched out in intolerable pain. On the cross those feet which had

93

carried him from place to place ministering to the needs of men were riveted fast with spikes. Again and again our Lord had preached and incarnated forgiving compassion. Yet on the cross he was the object of pitiless cruelty. He had offered the multitudes eternal life as a free gift. Yet on the cross the Prince of life was horribly put to death. Throughout his short life our Lord had manifested unwearying love. Yet on the cross he was rewarded with unmerited hate. And that hate cost our Saviour indescribable agony of heart.

But even that was not all Christ endured. Besides the agony of body and heart, there was his indescribable agony of spirit. Thus in words of bottomless depth Paul writes: "God hath made him to be sin for us who knew no sin; that we might be made the righteousness of God in him" (2 Cor. 5:21). What happened, then, on Calvary? Bear in mind that whenever we talk about the cross we are skirting the edge of an abyss; our human language breaks down under the weight of inexpressible truth. On Calvary Jesus Christ was made sin. Who can fathom what that experience cost him? We know that in his holiness he abhorred evil, drawing back from it in horror. We know that in his moral perfection he could see sin in all of its revolting hideousness as we cannot possibly see it. We know that in his divine sensitivity he could feel the crushing weight of sin as we cannot possibly feel it. He could taste all of the nauseating foulness of sin as we cannot possibly taste it. That was why he prayed, "If it be possible, let this cup pass from me"—that cup in all its nauseating foulness. Yet at the cross he lifted that cup and drank it to the dregs. He became sin.

Our Lord's reaction to sin can perhaps be partially understood if we take some of our own reactions and multiply them by infinity. I recall, for instance, that years ago as a pastor I visited a certain hospital regularly, and among its patients were two men who were dying of a malignancy that had attacked their faces. Week after week as I visited them, I was driven to ask God for grace in order to camouflage my feelings. Or think of Henry Drummond, the scientist-preacher of Scotland who came to the United States under the sponsorship of D. L. Moody. He was extremely popular as a college lecturer, and after his meetings students would invariably request personal help. One day after a long series of such conferences, Drummond was in his room with his head bowed upon his hands. A friend came in, glanced at him, and exclaimed, "Why Henry, what's the matter? Are you sick?" Drummond looked up and replied, "Yes, I'm sick. I'm sick of sin! How does God stand it?" God's endurance of man's sin is indeed a mystery. But there is a far greater mystery than that. Why was Jesus Christ willing to become sin for us?

When Jesus Christ became sin—and I scarcely know how to put this into human language—he became a spiritual derelict. He was abandoned by his Father. The eternal communion of triune deity was broken at that point in time, as the Son cried out, "My God, My God, why hast thou forsaken Me?" Dare we say it? In that hour our Lord must have experienced what it is to suffer a lost eternity. But why did he suffer so? Why did he endure such agony of body and heart and spirit? He did it not because of external pressure or cosmic necessity or inescapable fate. No, he did it solely because he loved us.

Let us consider Calvary, however, from the perspective of God the Father, and perhaps we will then be able to see something more of its glory as the time-abiding, heart-assuring, all-sufficient revelation of divine love. In the 53rd chapter of Isaiah there is a prophecy which is absolutely bafflling: "Yet it pleased the Lord to bruise him; he hath put him to grief; when thou shalt make his soul an offering for sin, he shall see his seed, he shall prolong his days, and the pleasure of the Lord shall prosper in his hands." Does this verse mean what it seems to say? Did God the Father put God the Son to grief? Was God the Father pleased to kill God the Son? That plunges thought into chaos. God the Father is not a heartless monster. God the Father is not a sadist who delights in torture. God the Father is not an emotional blank. God the Father is not a psychopath, a Mind without a Heart! Yet the text declares that God the Father was pleased to bruise God the Son. How can we possibly explain this?

A counter question must be raised. Can we believe that the love of God the Father for God the Son was inferior to the love which David the father had for Absalom his son? By no means! It was infinitely greater. But David wept over treacherous Absalom, "My son, my son, would that I had died for thee!" Then how must we suppose that God the Father felt when God the Son was dying on the cross? Why not assert it boldly? The heart of God the Father must have broken with the heart of God the Son.

Ian Maclaren's unforgettable book about life in the Scotch highlands, *Beside the Bonnie Brier-Bush*, introduces us to Lachlan Campbell, a Presbyterian elder of the old school, a man of rigid character and inflexible principles. After his wife died, he did not really know how to bring up his young daughter Flora. Lachlan was so severe and harsh that the girl simply could not tolerate her home. So one night, leaving a note behind, she ran away to Edinburgh. In his unbending righteousness and

Highland simplicity, Lachlan was sure that she had embarked upon a wicked life. So he opened the family Bible in which he had proudly inscribed his genealogy and scratched out Flora's name. I need not rehearse all the details of the story here. It will be enough to say that a godly neighbor, Margaret Howe, succeeded in convincing Lachlan that his daughter had run away just because she craved excitement and longed for a mother's understanding. And so at last Flora was welcomed back. But immediately after Flora ran away, Margaret accidently saw the genealogy in Lachlan's Bible—and, though Flora's name had indeed been scratched out, the ink had been blurred by her father's tears. To give up his daughter broke Lachlan's heart.

How must we suppose God the Father felt when God the Son died on the cross? Take the central truth of Ian Maclaren's story, lift it to an infinite level, and answer that question. What was the reaction of God the Father when God the Son became sin? What did God the Father do when the fractured law of the moral universe was vindicated on the cross? What did God the Father do? May we suppose that God the Father remained an impressive spectator? Was God a compassionless icicle, watching it all with sadistic delight? No! No! No! God the Father must have wept with a broken heart! But why did God the Father and God the Son undergo such agony? The New Testament gives just one reason. God suffered like that because of love for you and me and the whole lost world. Only through God's redemptive travail could his creative purposes at last be brought to fulfillment, and God was willing to pay the price.

That is why we glory in the cross. That is why we make Calvary our boast. That is why we are sure that back of all history and nature there is a God of infinite love. That is why, in our world of darkness, we seek to share the message of the cross, the message that floods the darkness with the light of redemptive love.

11

Surprise!

Mark 16:1–8

It is always nice to welcome the Easter season. It signals the return of spring with its happy festivals and its parades of flowers and clothes and boats and all manner of things. It is a lovely time of year.

And as for Easter Day itself—it is great to escape from the ordinary for a while, and leave our burdens and troubles and fears and failures all behind and go to church for an hour to enter that never-never land of Easter dreams.

All of which is to miss the point, of course. Before ever we go to an Easter service we ought to gather those very fears and failures and troubles and burdens and take them with us, for the suffering of the cross, the death and entombment of Jesus Christ, and the working of the resurrection power of God is for something more than a

Robert E. Goodrich, Jr., Bishop, The United Methodist Church.

festival of spring with its clever animals and Easter egg trees!

Most of us have made an accomodation to some of the materialism which now surrounds the Easter season, and even go along with the incredible myth of rabbits which lay eggs, colored and decorated. But sometimes things do seem to go too far. Last year I clipped from the newspaper in one Texas city an announcement from the public library of the special activities planned for the children of the city. "The Easter bunnies and their helpers are coming to tell stories to all the small-fry at the library units . . . Children will be given paper Easter eggs to decorate and hang on the Easter Egg Trees (!) . . . Library assistants will be dressed as Easter bunnies. A live rabbit and parakeet will be making stops along with the bunnies at the mobile branch units . . . All librarians will be in Easter costumes (meaning make-like rabbit dress . . .)"

Now I know we are dealing with some sacred traditions in all of this—sacred to our secular society!—but it is disturbing that nowhere is there any mention of what Easter really means. It suggests that we are training our children to be able to give their affirmation in some such words as, "I believe in Easter eggs and bunny rabbits and parakeets and colored cut-outs . . . etc." And that's not much of a faith to prepare them for the facing of this world in which they must live. Presumably, however, that is about as far as many adults get today.

Maybe all of this seems super-tragic this year because the world needs the Easter message more than ever. In fact, for you and me, this ought to be the most important Easter we have ever known.

Of course, I'll confess that this is the conviction I have

100

had about every Easter I have known. Maybe this is the way we *ought* to feel each year.

We had a coach at Centenary College who had the gift of making us feel that way about each game. Actually, this was about the only hope we had one year: we didn't have much talent but we learned to cry a lot. I recall one year when we played SMU in Dallas. We stayed at a downtown hotel in those days and that is where we had our pre-game meeting. The coach gave his talk and we had some testimonials from the players, and the tears began to flow, and soon we were ready to swear that we were ready to die for the honor of old Centenary that afternoon. Which we almost did! SMU beat us 33 to 3. I've always felt that we just didn't have enough strength to play a decent game that afternoon: we were emotionally exhausted before we ever got to the stadium.

The next year, however, we had some additional talent, and the coach had perfected his pre-game technique to the point that we did feel each game was absolutely essential: we had to win. And we did, all eleven games.

And maybe this is the way we *should* feel about Easter, especially as Christians: that each one is the most important Easter the world has ever known.

It certainly could be true this year.

After all, there are more dead people than ever before. I am not thinking now about the thriving cemetery business and the ever expanding graveyards. I am thinking about the living dead—those who breathe and move and walk the streets but are indifferent to life and its values. The drop-outs, the cop-outs, the sick-outs, the think-outs, and all the others who have given up on life to lead an apathetic existence. Somewhere I read a description by Dr. Eric Fromm: "A man sits in front of a bad television program and doesn't know that he is bored; he joins the rat race of commerce, where personal worth is measured in terms of market values, and is not aware of his anxiety. Ulcers speak louder than words.

"Theologians and philosophers have been saying for a century that God is dead, but what we confront now is the possibility that *man is dead,* transformed into a thing, a producer, a consumer, an idolater of other things . . ." There are more of the living dead today than ever before.

Furthermore, the thingification of man is proceeding at a rapid rate. More and more the dignity of personhood is being stolen away from us. Big brothers keep their books on us! We're things to be manipulated and used. Their spies are enrolled in schools and are present in churches and church conferences. Years ago I learned some lines from a one-act opera by Gian Carlo Menotti, *The Consul:*

> Your name is a number;
> Your story's a case;
> Your hopes are on file!

Then the words were a nightmarish dream: today they are too much a reality for we are classified and catalogued—thingified!

And added to these are the secret personal fears and burdens and anxieties which all of us have.

So this may be the most important Easter ever for us because none of these are to be left behind when we come to its celebration. It is not a momentary escape into some dream-land. Easter is real! And Easter is for now!

Read again the record of that first Easter according to Mark's gospel (Mark 16:1-8). There are three rather shocking surprises which have to do with us.

102

Scene one. Mary Magdalene and the other women were on their way to the tomb. They planned to anoint the body of Jesus for burial. Suddenly they remembered the great stone which sealed the entrance to the tomb. "Who will roll it away for us?" they asked. As they came near the place, however, they looked up. And the stone had already been rolled back. This was the first great surprise of that magnificent morning.

Isn't this a picture of the way it is with so many of our own anxieties and worries which we allow to steal away the strength of life? We imagine some difficulty out there ahead of us. We know it will be too much for us and we begin to cry, "How can I handle it? What am I going to do?"

But as time moves us closer to the moment of crisis, how often we discover that our worries have been useless. It would be interesting if we were to make an honest list of all the things we have been worrying about during the past week, to keep the list for six months, and then see just how much energy we had wasted in needless anxiety.

I once knew of a woman who kept a "worry-table." She wanted to check the facts for she realized how much of her life she was wasting in almost constant worrying. And at the end of a period of time she came up with these results: 40 percent of them never happened; 30 percent of them concerned old decisions which she could not alter in any way; 12 percent of them were due to criticism directed at her by others, mostly made by insecure persons, and having no validity; 10 percent of her worries had to do with her health, which only deteriorated the more she worried; *only 8 percent were legitimate,* for life does have some real problems.

103

The Easter scene ought to mark a new beginning for us in this regard, for remember the women on the way to the tomb were worrying about a stone which had already been rolled away!

Furthermore, in their concern they had not reckoned with the power of God. It is a strange thing that none of them, and none of the disciples, none of the friends of Jesus, seem to have been expecting anything other than a body, cold and dead in the grave. They did not count God in at all.

And this is the way it often is with us in our worries and concerns, especially in regard to what we call death. In the midst of our desolation and grief, there is little evidence that we have really included God in the event.

Dr. Daniel Poling once wrote of his last visit with his mother out in Oregon. She was quite ill and elderly. As he prepared to leave to return to his office across the continent in New York, he sat with her for one final hour. When at last he started to leave the room, she called to him: "Dan, if I'm not here when you return, you'll know where to find me." Those were the last words he heard his mother speak, and he did know where to find her.

It does make a difference when God is reckoned with. This is true about all our worries and concerns and anxieties about the things we must meet, or what may happen to those we love.

Scene two, according to Mark. When the women entered the tomb, there was a young man in a white robe. "Do not be afraid, don't be frightened," he said to them. "You are looking for Jesus who was nailed to the cross. He is not here. He has risen!" Surprise!

The guards would have put it differently. They would

have said, "He is not here. He has *escaped!*" But the Easter word is, "He has risen. He is set free from the jail in which they had thought to keep him good and dead forever." Risen! It meant that a living Christ had been set free to be with them . . . and with us.

This ought to be so much easier for us to accept and believe than it was for Mary Magdalene and the other women, or the disciples, or any of those who loved him in that day. After all, we have two thousand years of proof, as it were. We have the witness of unnumbered persons through the ages who have found it so, who have known the presence of a living Christ. We have the evidence of millions of persons who have been changed, made new, resurrected by his power.

He is risen. He is set free!

Halford Luccock had an experience which gave a little different turn to these words. He was waiting two hours on a late train in a little village one Sunday afternoon. As he walked the square, about the only thing he found open was the post office. Inside he found the usual art gallery—the pictures of men wanted for robbing the mails and other crimes. Rewards were offered for their capture. Then his imaginative mind went to work, and he pictured a poster with the face of Jesus upon it, and underneath such words as, "The Most Dangerous Man In The World Is At Large, Loose, Free."

And He is dangerous, even to those who put a sign on their door "Do Not Disturb," for they want to get on with their business, undisturbed by matters of honor and truth and ethics and moral principles and justice! He is dangerous to the status quo, for he is set free to go into ghettos and slave quarters to stir the people and lift them to their feet, awakening in them a sense of dignity and worth in the sight of God. He is a constant threat to those who would make persons into things to be used.

Playboy's first "playmate" was Marilyn Monroe whose nude photograph Hugh Hefner purchased for $300 to start his magazine in 1953. The *deal* was like the shadow of the future, for her tragic life ended in suicide. And the one statement she had made which best explains the act was, "I never felt like a person . . . only an object."

In the Christian viewpoint, the essence of sin is to treat persons as things. And in the continuing struggle of things or people, truth or lies, good or evil, Jesus Christ is loose and is someone to deal with.

The risen Lord is a judgment upon more than death! He is set free to be in our midst to bless and help and keep and strengthen. But also he is free to be the disturbing presence among those who would destroy the dignity of those whom God has made, and whom he loves!

Scene three. The young man in the white robe, presiding over the empty tomb, said to the women, "Go and tell his disciples, and Peter, that he is going before you into Galilee; you will see him there as he told you." The only one of the disciples he mentions by name is Peter, as if he were to receive special handling. Surprise!

Why was Peter singled out among the disciples? After all, he was the one who had denied Jesus three times there in the courtyard after the arrest. He had claimed he did not even know the man Jesus, had disowned any relationship to him. Peter, the one who had vowed that even if all the other disciples fell away, he would stand faithful. But now he was Peter the failure, and in that hour must have been suffering the shame and remorse of it all.

106

But all of this only meant that Peter, more than any of the others, needed the assurance that Jesus had not turned from him or given up on him. Tell the disciples . . . and Peter who needs the message in a special way.

Doesn't this say something important to most of us? How often we have been the ones who were going to stand up for him and live our Christian faith, regardless of the pressures and yet how easily we slipped into compromise and even denial. There may have been times when we even thought we could be a martyr for his sake, but when the showdown came our courage collapsed. How often we have felt like crying, "My God, why didn't I stand up for him? Why didn't I speak up for my Christian faith and principles? Why was I silent when a word, two words, might have made such a difference?"

So we made a miserable mess of it all and deep inside we felt the loneliness of failure. But now comes the Easter message: "Tell the disciples . . . and Peter." Especially, Peter, the failure! This means that we can take heart. We can walk away from what we have been, for the Master of forgiveness is also the Master of another chance and the creator of twice-born men.

> He breaks the power of cancelled sin,
> He sets the prisoner free.

Surprise! Easter is far more than a message of life beyond the grave. Easter is for now! It speaks to our habits of worry and anxiety and calls us to more confident living day by day: God has surprising ways of helping us to be equal to that experience or task which we fear.

Easter is the assurance of a living Christ—a disturbing presence for those who violate God's love and his creation, but a comforting presence bringing strength to those who are open to him.

And Easter is a special message for those who have failed. Our failure need never be final for God never gives up on us and his love never says farewell.

Easter is for now!

12

The Resurrection
and Human Behavior

Galatians 2:19–20, Romans 6:1–4, Romans 8:38,39

The resurrection of our Lord Jesus Christ is a pattern
for human action, although it is more often the subject
for idle speculation about the mechanics of the event. My
concern is with the resurrection as a vital principle of
day-to-day human behavior as we cope with the grimy
fears that make cowards of us all and as we make ethical
decisions in the face of overwhelming threats to our basic
existence.

In the three Scripture references printed above, we find
that the Apostle Paul participates in the resurrection of
Jesus Christ himself, and in doing so finds a paradigm for
the resolution of human conflict and the development of
a spiritually enlivened ethical freedom and responsibility.
The resurrection for the Apostle Paul and for us should
and can be the driving dynamic of our daily behavior.

Wayne E. Oates, professor of psychology of religion, Southern Baptist
Theological Seminary.

According to these three Scripture references, we can identify three major ethical problems for which the resurrection becomes both the solution and a "more excellent" way of life.

The resurrection and bondage of the law

As he wrote to the Galatians, the Apostle Paul found them lapsing back into the elaborate legal system of Judaism. His patience was tried to its limits as he wrote to them. They were relying on new moons and sabbaths instead of participation in the faith that Christ was risen from the dead and that he had set them free from all this. For freedom Christ had set them free, but they were now becoming entangled again in the yoke of bondage. In response to this, the Apostle Paul said that he had died to the law because it had killed him. Yet he nevertheless had been enlivened through faith in the risen Christ. Christ as Spirit now filled his life and had taken the place of the old self that was in bondage to the law. He now lived according to this faith in the living Christ, not according to the law.

Contemporary Christians are deeply tempted to transmute the codes and customs of their particular form of institutional religion into an infallible law. For them it is not enough to participate in the sustained obedience to the Spirit of Christ. Specific letters of law, belief, and practice are set out that take the place of this participation in the celebration of the resurrected Christ's presence. Young children are collared with this yoke of bondage with such zeal and vigor that they feel themselves to be outside the pale of redemption when as young people they begin to question the rules, laws, pet ways of saying things, and break loose for freedom from these. Parental

110

and pastoral authority are often used to demand strict obedience to customs and codes that vary widely even within the ranks of one denomination of Christians.

For example, I as a Southern Baptist can swim in water that is not over five feet deep. I am six feet tall. Therefore, swimming is not a matter of great importance to me as it is to my sons who are quite talented at scuba diving. Yet, we as a family can go to an assembly of Baptists at Florida locations and hear announcements that all the boys and girls who want to go swimming at the beach should be ready at 1:30 that afternoon to take a bus together. During the same summer we would go to Ridgecrest and see strict rules that boys and girls were not allowed to swim together! Or, another example: as a professor at the Southern Baptist Seminary, I have lived through one effort after another to require the man who teaches to agree literally to the statement of faith written by someone else whom he does not even know personally.

These are bondages to the peccadillos of behavior and to the verbal deifications of the thoughts of men. Persons in other denominations can smile with superiority at such examples as I have quoted. However, close examination of any group of Christians will reveal this bondage to the law.

The Apostle Paul took the resurrection seriously enough to say that such literalism kills the Spirit and that he had died to the law. In spite of this death, the living God had brought the resurrected Christ alive within him. It was not he that was behaving, but Christ in him. He lived, therefore, not by the letter of the law but in the faith that Christ had been raised from the dead and was enlivening his whole life with freedom from bondage to such legalism.

If the resurrection is a pattern of action in human behavior, then the presence of the resurrected Christ in our lives takes the place of straining at gnats and swallowing camels over the compulsive rituals others expect of us. Worse still we can be free of half-expecting them of ourselves. This is where our inner conflict arises. With the freedom brought us by the living Christ we can live our lives "readily and not out of constraint" as we respond spontaneously to the tutelage of the Spirit from within and to the appearing of the Lord Jesus Christ in the hurts and wounds of other people around us.

Rebellion against the law for its own sake is self-destructive. Such rebellion is what we could call "runaway creativity" at best. However, rebellion against the law through dying to it, being risen in Christ Jesus, and walking in faith in him who loved us and gave himself for us unshackles us from the bondage to the law at the same time it puts us in touch with a higher source of moral strength and courage. We have no longer a spirit of fear, but of power, and of love and of self-control.

The resurrection anad the temptation to libertinism

What has been said thus far is only part of the whole truth about the resurrection and human behavior. Paul dealt with another kind of Christian as he wrote to the Romans. They believed they had been freed from the law, that grace was abundant, and that the more they sinned, the more God would forgive them. They threw caution to the winds and became real libertines, doing as they pleased. "Anything goes!" seemed to be their motto.

It is not very difficult for us to find this same mentality among Christians today. For example a young couple wanted to get married. The "Jesus freak" groom was ter-

112

ribly upset with his prospective Episcopalian mother-in-law because she wanted to serve champagne at the wedding reception. However, he felt that the fact that his girl friend and he had been living together sexually for three months was quite okay. Jesus understood. Why didn't everyone else? None of this was a secret. Their circle of friends knew it, accepted it, and talked easily of it. Therefore, don't accuse me of betraying "confidences." It didn't even come to me in confidence. It was common knowledge.

The Apostle Paul again turned to the resurrection of Jesus Christ as a pattern for dealing with his libertarian opponents. The resurrected Christ again became the source of moral energy, direction, and patterning for behavior. Paul said that in identifying ourselves with Christ we have died to sin. We were buried with Christ into his baptism. We were raised as he was raised from the dead, and we now walk in the newness of life. The discipline of desire becomes as important as the achievement of freedom from the law. We have been united in a death to sin as Christ was who became sin in order that we might become the righteousness of God in him. Therefore, we are united with him in his resurrection. The old self of sin and self-serving has been crucified and the new self of being alive to God in Christ lifts us out of the bondage to sin.

The ethical life of the Christian, therefore, is lifted out of the realm of rules and thrust into the realm of an intimate personal relationship to Christ. The passions of the mind of the Christian are focused upon Christ being formed within us and expressed through us in the kind of things he did and the kind of mind that he had in him. The passions of the mind are not focused on the orgies

113

of self-pleasing. Freedom from the law was brought about through dying and being resurrected with Christ. Responsible behavior is brought about in one and the same act of dying to sin and being raised to walk in the newness of life.

The resurrection and the threat of separation

The bondage of the law, the chaos of unlimited desire, and the threat of being separated from one's very being and from Christ seem to be some of the most important mainsprings of Christian behavior. The Apostle Paul raises the deepest question in our third text. If our freedom from the law and from sin depends entirely upon our participation in the life, death, and resurrection of Christ, what would happen if we should be separated from him? This is the great threat that hangs over us at all times. We long to have durable relationships to each other. We are anxiety-laden when we have to leave those whom we love or when we are left by them. In the natural course of things, we are called upon to leave father and mother, brothers, sons and daughters, houses, lands, and our own lives, too. The rippage of relationships is painful, and we die a little each time we lose someone. From the vantage point of Christ, it is not enough to say that we die a little. We *are,* as Paul says, killed all the day long. But this is not enough. We are also raised to walk in the newness of life.

The resurrection of Christ, then, is the beginning of hope in the face of separation. As for whether anything can separate us from Christ, who is the moral energizer of our lives as well as the moral liberator from bondage to the law, nothing can separate us from the love he has for us. This is the security of the person who participates

114

in his resurrection. In human behavior, the resurrection of Christ stands for the reality that a relationship once really established cannot be broken. He will not forsake us and we will never be alone again.

In a world in which we are no longer concerned with the little peculiarities of the law nor have any desire to do other than abide in Christ, rivers of sorrow do seem to overflow. We, to change the figure of speech a bit, feel sometimes that a fourteen-foot tidal wave will succumb us. We ask the basic question Paul asked, "Can we really be separated from Christ?" The promise of his resurrection is that this relationship cannot and will not be broken. *Nothing* can separate us!

13

Victory That Lasts

Ah, Golgotha! unhappy Golgotha!
The Lord of Glory here beneath a curse is lying
He hangs upon th' accursed tree,
Who shall the World Redeemer be;
The Lord Who heaven and earth created.
By earth is now reviled and hated:
The sinless, lo, for sin is dying;
With stricken soul the sight I see.

J.S. Bach
Passion According to St. Matthew

The heart-breaking Friday finally ends; nothing goes on
and on without at least an ending. Then for the disciples,
the lonely days of failure and regret settle over them. On
the first day of the week the women gather at dawn to
arrange for as decent a burial as their money would allow,

Earl Palmer, Senior Minister, First Presbyterian Church of Berkeley,
California.

but what they found at the graveyard on that early morning was to be told by men to one another and to their children throughout all of the centuries: the tomb was empty. The heavy stone at the doorway was rolled back. The small Roman guard was asleep, and a young man, a total stranger to the women, was there. He announced to them that Jesus Christ was alive. They did not believe even that the grave was empty, let alone the report of Christ's triumph over death! After all, why should they?

Death has the last word over the great as well as the small. But the fact is that within a few days of that first day of the new week of man, these disciples, even Thomas, were sure enough of the victory of Jesus Christ to risk their lives on it. They told the world that Jesus had challenged the two foes that we men cannot handle—our sins and our death—and that he had conquered each.

Though the battle won on Easter day is dramatic, the resurrection of Jesus as an event is a quiet one. Our Lord's victory over death bears the same reserve about it that marks his whole ministry. The encounters of Christ with his disciples after the resurrection are brief and few. What Jesus does not do after that decisive day is to prove himself to his contestors: neither the leaders of the Sanhedrin nor the Roman officials, nor the wealthy Herodians experienced any embarrassing encounters with the risen Christ.

Apparently, as far as they were concerned, their coalition against Jesus had been successful. The only hints of possible danger to them arise in the unaccountable rumors, the fearlessness on the part of the disciples, the spreading joy and excitement among crowds of people who listened to the bold message of Peter, James, and John. And there was the fact of the empty grave.

117

The truth of Christ's victory over death is affirmed by the disciples through the New Testament documents and preaching; it is attested by what happens in the lives of the disciples. They witnessed to the resurrection in various ways, some direct and some indirect. What happens in the lives of the family of men and women who will wager their lives on the message of the gospel of Christ is remarkable. Their total lack of interest in building shrines, their boldness, their confidence in the Word of Life, the moral straightness of their message and the contagiousness of the faith as indirect evidences are profoundly impressive.

Our accustomed methods of proving a thing one way or another are here confronted with a staggering and new event, an event where our primary technical evidence is so uninteresting. One empty tomb is like any other empty tomb. Christ's actual victory over death is only proven in any lasting way by the authentication of God himself. This confirming of the witness of the first century disciples is the result of the ministry of the Holy Spirit in men and women's lives. The triumph of our Lord Jesus Christ is a fact that we are called by God to wager on, and it is God who makes the triumph concrete, personal, universal, and actual to us.

If the event of Easter is true, then what are the results for us today? I want to point up two implications: first, the way that I look at the world and my own self as a part of the world is permanently altered. Because of the resurrection of Jesus Christ, death has lost its terrorizing grip over the created order, and I no longer need to be preoccupied by it. Not only that, but in a positive sense, the world and my own life have a new source for meaning now. Christ has validated this existence of mine.

118

Christ asserted a finality more lasting and more important than fear, sin, despair, inky black hollowness, grey endings, and death. These old fears and dangers are not as final as we once thought. The result of a new finality becomes the basis for my life now. There is a greater power at work. The freedom to live is stronger than the coalitions of sin which destroy. Love at work is greater than the wrath of man. The Lord of love and life is more durable than the forces we once thought were so complete and unending. Therefore, on this side of Easter I look at the world in a whole new way. When the value of my daily existence is confirmed, I am set free with a motivation and a mission to live out the implications of Christ's death and resurrection in every direction.

Second, Easter has confirmed the meaning and authority of the ministry of Jesus Christ. The word and work of our Lord are validated once and for all. This is of decisive importance because it means that when Jesus makes the promise of forgiveness to a thief on the cross, when he promises forgiveness to us, when he pronounces hope, and when he calls men to follow him as the way, the truth, and the life, I know that because of the victory of Easter, his promises, his pronouncements, his authority will hold. His words are not the kindly sentiments of a good but ultimately powerless man, but rather the words of the Lord. Otherwise, do I dare build upon his promises, wager on his character? Do I dare spell out his ethical challenges to my life in a world like ours? Do I dare to believe that in the twentieth century Jesus Christ knows my name? Do I dare believe that Jesus Christ could possibly be contemporary to me?

Because of the actualness of Easter, the answer is yes! Go right ahead and build upon the words of Jesus Christ as if they are true, as if they hold ultimate weight, as if they still work, as if when life depends upon their trustworthiness they are worthy of that dependence. Go right ahead, because Jesus Christ, who made the promises, is alive!

14

He Always
Sneaks Up on Us

The most beautiful experiences so often take us by surprise—they sneak up on us. I recall asking folks one Sunday morning to greet one another before eating the bread or drinking the cup in the service of communion. It could even be a time of healing and reaffirmation among us, I suggested. There was a flurry of movement as folks reached out to greet one another. I started back to greet an older member whose wife had passed away a week or two before. He had not worshiped with us for a long time, and now he was sitting alone nursing his grief. But our son Joel, then a senior in high school and serving as a deacon, caught me by the arm as I moved out to speak to Bill. He looked me in the eye and simply said, "Dad, in the name of Christ, I love you." What an unforgettable gift! And so unexpected. It filled that whole service with joy!

Roger Fredrikson, Minister, First Baptist Church, Sioux Falls, South Dakota.

And recently I was walking down the hallway of a hotel and thought I heard music that sounded familiar. It turned out to be a cleaning lady humming "How Great Thou Art." All I could do was stop and listen for a moment. And then I asked her about it. "Oh," she said, "I became a Christian a couple of weeks ago. Billy Graham was preaching here, and one night I knew the message was for me. That night I gave my heart to Christ." Imagine stumbling into all that in a hotel corridor!

Or how can I ever forget a visit to the Moscow Baptist Church? In the midst of so much that is drab and dull and organized, here were people gathered to praise God and to rejoice in his love—a mighty foretaste of what is to come. It made no difference that they were packed together—over two thousand of them, and so many of them standing—or that the service lasted over two hours. They had waited all week for this experience of worship. No wonder many of them wept as they heard the word or joined in prayer or song.

How amazing that after fifty years of Russian communism people should be gathering for this kind of worship. After all, the official line has been that this is sheer nonsense—at best a myth. And all through the years there has been bitter persecution or at best the restricted tolerance of any talk or worship of God. By all normal standards the church should have been dead. Yet here they were singing hymns, praising God, and baptizing believers.

And this is what Easter is all about! Here God completely outflanked us. As Peter cried out in that first sermon preached on the day of Pentecost, "Death could not hold him." We had assumed that death was so final. That is really supposed to be the end! But we hadn't really reckoned on what God was up to! Now we know!

We can never really grasp the power of Easter until we know the tragedy and darkness that came before it. Jesus' dream had been a lovely thing—all that talk about his kingdom of love and peace. And everything he did made that kingdom so real—healing the sick, casting out demons, and loving the outcasts the way he did. But in the end it was crushed, all wiped out.

And his death was not some quiet, little normal affair. The evil forces were drawn together in an unholy alliance to do him in—Caiaphas and the Sanhedrin, Pilate doing business with Herod, and the treachery of Judas. And we are spared none of the anguish or brutality of his death. It is all there in the Gospels—the cries and the noise and finally the muffled sobs of his followers. Now it is over.

Matthew tells of the arrangements made by Joseph of Arimathea so the body could be put in his new grave, with the stone and guard at the entrance, at the insistence of some of the Pharisees. Luke says, "The crowd went home beating their breasts." And John says it was so obvious Jesus was dead the soldiers didn't need to break his legs. They stabbed his side with a spear and "at once there was a flow of blood and water."

And that was it! From our side!

But God had other plans. He moved in right in the middle of all the funeral arrangements—the women hurrying early in the morning to finish the burial. There hadn't been time for that on that awful Friday afternoon. Otherwise the Sabbath would have been desecrated.

But the living Lord broke all that up! And once those crushed, scattered disciples became aware he was really alive they went running up and down the roads shouting it out! "Christ is alive!"

The women were utterly overwhelmed that the grave

was empty. And when the news reached Peter and John, they came running like a couple of school boys. Two disciples were amazed when the stranger sharing their hospitality took the bread to bless it, and it turned out he was the resurrected Lord. What a place and time for the surprise to break in—at the table while the food was being blessed! No wonder they hurried back to Jerusalem. Their hearts were burning and the news had to be shared.

And in John's Gospel we catch the wonder of God's surprise in a variety of situations. The women find the tomb empty—and can only affirm that Christ is not where he is "supposed" to be. Then Mary stands weeping in the garden and assumes that the One beside her is the gardener. But when he speaks her name, with that familiar tone—then she knows. Now she can only worship him. And later that night the disciples have gathered in a room in the city with the door locked. Surely there must have been a great deal of discussion about all these wild rumors. But then he is there—the risen One—and speaks again that familiar greeting, "Shalom. My peace be with you." And they are filled with incredible joy!

But Thomas, one of the twelve, is not there and insists he will not accept the words of the others unless he can see and touch the living Christ. And he speaks for a thousand stubborn, practical men who say, "You've got to show me." And our Lord appears in response to that persistent yearning. He even points to the wounds. This is no apparition, no ghostly appearance. This is the risen Jesus. Thomas can only cry out, "My Lord and my God." That is all any of us can do.

And that is God's side of the story. When all our human resources have given out and we are at the end of everything, then Jesus makes his appearance. "The human extremity becomes the divine opportunity." The resurrection is God's answer to human sin and death. Our rebellion on Friday calls forth God's mighty act on Sunday. That is his answer. And we come to discover in some mysterious way he was in it all the time.

And while the resurrection is an event—a happening at a particular time and place—it is more than that! It is a cosmic, eternal victory that changes everything. The resurrection means the defeat of the forces of evil. New possibilities for all creation are now opened up. This is why Paul can cry out, "When anyone is united to Christ, there is a new world; the old order has gone, and a new order has already begun" (2 Cor. 5:17, NEB). We can live in the resurrection power through the Spirit today.

But a vast part of our world lives as if this had never happened. It is on the way to a funeral. How can anyone talk about life and hope? Look at our failures. They are all around us. Our proud pretensions—scientific, educational, political—have come tumbling down around us. Many of our hopes have been left in shambles. The decay of our inner cities, the breakdown of institutions, the filth and violence which spreads like a cancer, the old wars that drag on and the new wars that threaten to break out—is not all of this like an awesome graveyard?

Ingmar Bergman, one of the sensitive spirits of our time, has written about the "silence of God." We live in an awesome darkness, acting out our little part as if God were not around at all. And the deepest anguish of all this is the breakdown of the human spirit. The grim joylessness of life, the loss of all expectation, the exhausting drive to find some new fad or gimmick—all of this reveals an emptiness at the center of life. Is there any God around at all?

But there are stirrings. Rumors are going around.

Could it be a resurrection has taken place—only we don't quite dare believe it. Some people are celebrating because they know Christ is alive and among them. I remember a night in Minneapolis in a great old house a short time ago. I was meeting with a group of people who called themselves "the Church without walls." It was a beautiful, free night full of laughter and honesty. No question —Christ was there. Some of these people had known pain and rejection, but now they had tasted something new. They couldn't quite "buy" the institutional church, but they longed for some kind of community centered in Christ. So here they were.

And as I worshiped with them, I thought of all those places in the New Testament where it speaks of "the church in your house." And about all those groups I have heard about or know of that are meeting in offices and even warehouses, but most of them in homes. Here the life in Christ is celebrated!

Or there is Gary Bentley from Berkeley! He visited us some time ago, with his long hair and jeans and Bible— one of the Jesus people. At first we were suspicious, but then his authenticity won out, and we accepted him as a brother in Christ. He spoke of his community—the Bible studies and the witnessing and the joy of having all things in common. So many of them have gone the whole route —the drifting and confusion, the rebellion and the drugs —and then Christ! These are a strange, beautiful breed of people who know about the resurrection. How amazing that God should sneak up on us this way.

There is vast hunger and yearning for reality and truth on every hand. People are so tired of the old lies, the games, and the emptiness of all their possessions.

And they are not at all certain that institutionalized religion has the answer. But when talk gets around to Christ and the Spirit and the Bible—that's another matter. I must have had a hundred wistful, eager conversations in planes, restaurants, business men's luncheons—those places outside the church—about the meaning of it all. They want to know if Christ really makes a difference. Could it be that Easter is here and we aren't even aware of it?

New life is only possible because it is shared with us through an authentic Presence. Christ comes to us—as he did in the garden, or in that locked room, or to Thomas. There are a hundred times a day Christ is there—waiting, knocking, nudging. When that Presence is affirmed and worshiped, then whole new worlds open up. For then I become a "new creation."

His presence may come in a verse of Scripture, the line of a song, the witness of a friend. Or it may be an act of kindness, through the pain of a loss, or the discovery of my inadequacy. The resurrection has let the living Christ loose in all the world—and I must deal with him. He will slip up on me one way or another.

And the mystery of faith is when my eyes are opened so I see and hear him. This is a deeper capacity than reason—awakened only by the Spirit. For too many of us faith has been something we use when reason runs out. We assume we will use it now and then when we get in a pinch. Nothing could be further from the truth. Everything we do from planting a crop, to launching a new project, to opening ourselves to some friend is an act of faith. So when we hear our name called in the garden, and cry "Master" as Mary did, or hear the greeting "Shalom" in that locked room as the disciples did, our response is the word of faith. And it unlocks the door to the riches of the resurrection—forgiveness, belonging, everlasting life.

Wouldn't it be glorious if some of us became aware right now that "Christ is here!" "He's sneaked up on me." And all I can say in response is, "My Lord and my God."

After Mary

He made her want to live again,
Or keep on living,
When dying would be
Easier.

He made her want
The beautiful,
The good;
The *should* of life
Became her rock,
Not her stumbling-block.

He said she should go
And spread His word
Of love,
Just like the others,
The holy ones;
She, still dirty from
The street.
Yet He found her sweet enough,
In His God way,
To call her by her name,
To know her yearning heart,
And bid her go.

All the same He failed her;
How could it be right?
She sobbed.
He let them murder,
Stab and hammer
All the glory
From her sight.
He might have done otherwise,
But He let them leave Him
Hanging,
Brute-banging her
Against aloneness,
The soul's hell-wall.

All was lost, offensively;
And none could say,
Even in defense,
He did not let them do it.
"See you to it," He had said.
"See you to it."

She who had been called
So many names,
With such filthy variety,
Was left, bereft,
With nobody to call
Her by her name—
His way.
Other ways were insufficient,
Being deficient.

130

Nevertheless, when
He had let them do it,
And had gone,
She went calling,
Forlorning;
Mourning, mourning, mourning;
Found more nothing.
The deadhouse where
He let them put Him
Was a scooped-out eggshell.

Who cared about some *other* hell?
Tell the world
It didn't matter.
How could it
With Him gone—nowhere?
Nowhere.
There is, soul, *no where!*

Must not let frenzy rise . . .
Not wise.
O dear What's 'is name,
Why not?
To be done with it all,
To fall into oblivion . . .

Why *should* she care
If, where Celestia is considered,
It was decided He would die
In order that she (and also I)
Might live again one day?

But still,
If she could just remember
Anything He said,
Now He was dead—and gone.

"Go!
Go on—and on—and on."
Now? But where?
In this bleak unknowing
Unknown?

Also how,
Now He had gone?

And why?

From the deadhouse
She turned,
And knew this lump of dread,
Of bedded agony within,
More burdensome than
All the torturous
Devils He'd expelled
From her.

She turned.
And *there he was;*
Yet because she felt to self
So strangerly,
She supposed Him
Someone else.

132

From beyond the shell
Of earthness
He came gently, reverently,
And called her by her name.

Stepping over the small ash
Of her ember self
Into glory,
She gasped. She laughed!
Surcease,
Release,
Increase eternal!

Always after, she
Would find no horror
In spilled blood,
The grave,
Would even wave at death.
Trial and triumph
She judged the same.
The only thought
Of consequence was this:
Forever He would call
Her by her name.

O Lord, regarding me,
Who has denigrated self
So many times,
Name-calling,
There is no one to look
Into my heart,
To know me as I want to be.

Not even me.

Please!
Halt this deadhouse vigiling,
And after Mary,
Speed me to proclaim
Your wondrous love.

Oh, call me by my name!

Sallie Chesham